KNOW YOUR GOVERNMENT

The Immigration and Naturalization Service

The Immigration and Naturalization Service

Edward H. Dixon
and
Mark A. Galan

1523

CHELSEA HOUSE PUBLISHERS

On the cover: At a naturalization ceremony held at the Jefferson Memorial in Washington, D.C., on Liberty Weekend in 1986, aliens take the oath of citizenship and become American citizens with all the rights guaranteed by the Constitution.

Frontispiece: Illegal aliens wait to file their applications for the amnesty program of the Immigration Reform and Control Act of 1986.

Chelsea House Publishers
Editor-in-Chief: Nancy Toff
Executive Editor: Remmel T. Nunn
Managing Editor: Karyn Gullen Browne
Copy Chief: Juliann Barbato
Picture Editor: Adrian G. Allen
Art Director: Maria Epes
Manufacturing Manager: Gerald Levine

Know Your Government
Senior Editor: Kathy Kuhtz

Staff for THE IMMIGRATION AND NATURALIZATION SERVICE
Associate Editor: Scott Prentzas
Copy Editor: Michael Goodman
Editorial Assistant: Gregory R. Rodríguez
Picture Research: Dixon & Turner Associates, Inc.
Picture Coordinator: Melanie Sanford
Assistant Art Director: Loraine Machlin
Senior Designer: Noreen M. Lamb
Production Manager: Joseph Romano
Production Coordinator: Marie Claire Cebrián

First Printing

1   3   5   7   9   8   6   4   2

Library of Congress Cataloging-in-Publication Data

Dixon, Edward H.
  The Immigration and Naturalization Service / Edward H. Dixon and
Mark A. Galan.
    p.   cm.
  Bibliography: p.
  Includes index.
  Summary: Surveys the history of the Immigration and Naturalization Service and describes its structure, current functions and influence on American society.
    ISBN 1-55546-113-1.—ISBN 0-7910-0899-1 (pbk.)
    1. United States. Immigration and Naturalization Service—Juvenile literature.   2. United States—Emigration and immigration—Government policy— Juvenile literature.   [1. United States. Immigration and Naturalization Service.   2. Emigration and immigration.]   I. Galan, Mark A.
II. Title.   89-15733
JV6483.D59   1990   CIP
353.0081'7—dc20   AC

CONTENTS

Introduction   7

1 A Nation of Immigrants   15

2 Early Immigration to the United States   21

3 The Need for Regulation   35

    Feature Ellis Island—Gateway to America   46

4 Inside the INS   69

5 The INS Today   85

6 Keepers of the Flame   99

    Organizational Chart   102

    Glossary   104

    Selected References   106

    Index   107

KNOW YOUR GOVERNMENT

The American Red Cross

The Bureau of Indian Affairs

The Central Intelligence Agency

The Commission on Civil Rights

The Department of Agriculture

The Department of the Air Force

The Department of the Army

The Department of Commerce

The Department of Defense

The Department of Education

The Department of Energy

The Department of Health and
Human Services

The Department of Housing and
Urban Development

The Department of the Interior

The Department of Justice

The Department of Labor

The Department of the Navy

The Department of State

The Department of Transportation

The Department of the Treasury

The Drug Enforcement Administration

The Environmental Protection Agency

The Equal Employment
Opportunities Commission

The Federal Aviation Administration

The Federal Bureau of Investigation

The Federal Communications Commission

The Federal Government: How it Works

The Federal Reserve System

The Federal Trade Commission

The Food and Drug Administration

The Forest Service

The House of Representatives

The Immigration and Naturalization Service

The Internal Revenue Service

The Library of Congress

The National Aeronautics and Space
Administration

The National Archives and Records
Administration

The National Foundation on the Arts
and the Humanities

The National Park Service

The National Science Foundation

The Nuclear Regulatory Commission

The Peace Corps

The Presidency

The Public Health Service

The Securities and Exchange Commission

The Senate

The Small Business Administration

The Smithsonian

The Supreme Court

The Tennessee Valley Authority

The U.S. Arms Control and
Disarmament Agency

The U.S. Coast Guard

The U.S. Constitution

The U.S. Fish and Wildlife Service

The U.S. Information Agency

The U.S. Marine Corps

The U.S. Mint

The U.S. Postal Service

The U.S. Secret Service

The Veterans Administration

CHELSEA HOUSE PUBLISHERS

INTRODUCTION

Government: Crises of Confidence

Arthur M. Schlesinger, jr.

From the start, Americans have regarded their government with a mixture of reliance and mistrust. The men who founded the republic did not doubt the indispensability of government. "If men were angels," observed the 51st Federalist Paper, "no government would be necessary." But men are not angels. Because human beings are subject to wicked as well as to noble impulses, government was deemed essential to assure freedom and order.

At the same time, the American revolutionaries knew that government could also become a source of injury and oppression. The men who gathered in Philadelphia in 1787 to write the Constitution therefore had two purposes in mind. They wanted to establish a strong central authority and to limit that central authority's capacity to abuse its power.

To prevent the abuse of power, the Founding Fathers wrote two basic principles into the new Constitution. The principle of federalism divided power between the state governments and the central authority. The principle of the separation of powers subdivided the central authority itself into three branches—the executive, the legislative, and the judiciary—so that "each may be a check on the other." The *Know Your Government* series focuses on the major executive departments and agencies in these branches of the federal government.

The Constitution did not plan the executive branch in any detail. After vesting the executive power in the president, it assumed the existence of "executive departments" without specifying what these departments should be. Congress began defining their functions in 1789 by creating the Departments of State, Treasury, and War. The secretaries in charge of these departments made up President Washington's first cabinet. Congress also provided for a legal officer, and President Washington soon invited the attorney general, as he was called, to attend cabinet meetings. As need required, Congress created more executive departments.

Setting up the cabinet was only the first step in organizing the American state. With almost no guidance from the Constitution, President Washington, seconded by Alexander Hamilton, his brilliant secretary of the treasury, equipped the infant republic with a working administrative structure. The Federalists believed in both executive energy and executive accountability and set high standards for public appointments. The Jeffersonian opposition had less faith in strong government and preferred local government to the central authority. But when Jefferson himself became president in 1801, although he set out to change the direction of policy, he found no reason to alter the framework the Federalists had erected.

By 1801 there were about 3,000 federal civilian employees in a nation of a little more than 5 million people. Growth in territory and population steadily enlarged national responsibilities. Thirty years later, when Jackson was president, there were more than 11,000 government workers in a nation of 13 million. The federal establishment was increasing at a faster rate than the population.

Jackson's presidency brought significant changes in the federal service. He believed that the executive branch contained too many officials who saw their jobs as "species of property" and as "a means of promoting individual interest." Against the idea of a permanent service based on life tenure, Jackson argued for the periodic redistribution of federal offices, contending that this was the democratic way and that official duties could be made "so plain and simple that men of intelligence may readily qualify themselves for their performance." He called this policy rotation-in-office. His opponents called it the spoils system.

In fact, partisan legend exaggerated the extent of Jackson's removals. More than 80 percent of federal officeholders retained their jobs. Jackson discharged no larger a proportion of government workers than Jefferson had done a generation earlier. But the rise in these years of mass political parties gave federal patronage new importance as a means of building the party and of rewarding activists. Jackson's successors were less restrained in the distribu-

8

tion of spoils. As the federal establishment grew—to nearly 40,000 by 1861—the politicization of the public service excited increasing concern.

After the Civil War the spoils system became a major political issue. High-minded men condemned it as the root of all political evil. The spoilsmen, said the British commentator James Bryce, "have distorted and depraved the mechanism of politics." Patronage, by giving jobs to unqualified, incompetent, and dishonest persons, lowered the standards of public service and nourished corrupt political machines. Office-seekers pursued presidents and cabinet secretaries without mercy. "Patronage," said Ulysses S. Grant after his presidency, "is the bane of the presidential office." "Every time I appoint someone to office," said another political leader, "I make a hundred enemies and one ingrate." George William Curtis, the president of the National Civil Service Reform League, summed up the indictment. He said,

> The theory which perverts public trusts into party spoils, making public
> employment dependent upon personal favor and not on proved merit,
> necessarily ruins the self-respect of public employees, destroys the
> function of party in a republic, prostitutes elections into a desperate
> strife for personal profit, and degrades the national character by lower-
> ing the moral tone and standard of the country.

The object of civil service reform was to promote efficiency and honesty in the public service and to bring about the ethical regeneration of public life. Over bitter opposition from politicians, the reformers in 1883 passed the Pendleton Act, establishing a bipartisan Civil Service Commission, competitive examinations, and appointment on merit. The Pendleton Act also gave the president authority to extend by executive order the number of "classified" jobs—that is, jobs subject to the merit system. The act applied initially only to about 14,000 of the more than 100,000 federal positions. But by the end of the 19th century 40 percent of federal jobs had moved into the classified category.

Civil service reform was in part a response to the growing complexity of American life. As society grew more organized and problems more technical, official duties were no longer so plain and simple that any person of intelligence could perform them. In public service, as in other areas, the all-round man was yielding ground to the expert, the amateur to the professional. The excesses of the spoils system thus provoked the counter-ideal of scientific public administration, separate from politics and, as far as possible, insulated against it.

The cult of the expert, however, had its own excesses. The idea that administration could be divorced from policy was an illusion. And in the realm of policy, the expert, however much segregated from partisan politics, can

9

never attain perfect objectivity. He remains the prisoner of his own set of values. It is these values rather than technical expertise that determine fundamental judgments of public policy. To turn over such judgments to experts, moreover, would be to abandon democracy itself; for in a democracy final decisions must be made by the people and their elected representatives. "The business of the expert," the British political scientist Harold Laski rightly said, "is to be on tap and not on top."

Politics, however, were deeply ingrained in American folkways. This meant intermittent tension between the presidential government, elected every four years by the people, and the permanent government, which saw presidents come and go while it went on forever. Sometimes the permanent government knew better than its political masters; sometimes it opposed or sabotaged valuable new initiatives. In the end a strong president with effective cabinet secretaries could make the permanent government responsive to presidential purpose, but it was often an exasperating struggle.

The struggle within the executive branch was less important, however, than the growing impatience with bureaucracy in society as a whole. The 20th century saw a considerable expansion of the federal establishment. The Great Depression and the New Deal led the national government to take on a variety of new responsibilities. The New Deal extended the federal regulatory apparatus. By 1940, in a nation of 130 million people, the number of federal workers for the first time passed the 1 million mark. The Second World War brought federal civilian employment to 3.8 million in 1945. With peace, the federal establishment declined to around 2 million by 1950. Then growth resumed, reaching 2.8 million by the 1980s.

The New Deal years saw rising criticism of "big government" and "bureaucracy." Businessmen resented federal regulation. Conservatives worried about the impact of paternalistic government on individual self-reliance, on community responsibility, and on economic and personal freedom. The nation in effect renewed the old debate between Hamilton and Jefferson in the early republic, although with an ironic exchange of positions. For the Hamiltonian constituency, the "rich and well-born," once the advocate of affirmative government, now condemned government intervention, while the Jeffersonian constituency, the plain people, once the advocate of a weak central government and of states' rights, now favored government intervention.

In the 1980s, with the presidency of Ronald Reagan, the debate has burst out with unusual intensity. According to conservatives, government intervention abridges liberty, stifles enterprise, and is inefficient, wasteful, and arbitrary. It disturbs the harmony of the self-adjusting market and creates worse troubles than it solves. Get government off our backs, according to the popular cliché, and our problems will solve themselves. When government is necessary, let it be at the local level, close to the people. Above all, stop the inexorable growth of the federal government.

In fact, for all the talk about the "swollen" and "bloated" bureaucracy, the federal establishment has not been growing as inexorably as many Americans seem to believe. In 1949, it consisted of 2.1 million people. Thirty years later, while the country had grown by 70 million, the federal force had grown only by 750,000. Federal workers were a smaller percentage of the population in 1985 than they were in 1955—or in 1940. The federal establishment, in short, has not kept pace with population growth. Moreover, national defense and the postal service account for 60 percent of federal employment.

Why then the widespread idea about the remorseless growth of government? It is partly because in the 1960s the national government assumed new and intrusive functions: affirmative action in civil rights, environmental protection, safety and health in the workplace, community organization, legal aid to the poor. Although this enlargement of the federal regulatory role was accompanied by marked growth in the size of government on all levels, the expansion has taken place primarily in state and local government. Whereas the federal force increased by only 27 percent in the 30 years after 1950, the state and local government force increased by an astonishing 212 percent.

Despite the statistics, the conviction flourishes in some minds that the national government is a steadily growing behemoth swallowing up the liberties of the people. The foes of Washington prefer local government, feeling it is closer to the people and therefore allegedly more responsive to popular needs. Obviously there is a great deal to be said for settling local questions locally. But local government is characteristically the government of the locally powerful. Historically, the way the locally powerless have won their human and constitutional rights has often been through appeal to the national government. The national government has vindicated racial justice against local bigotry, defended the Bill of Rights against local vigilantism, and protected natural resources against local greed. It has civilized industry and secured the rights of labor organizations. Had the states' rights creed prevailed, there would perhaps still be slavery in the United States.

The national authority, far from diminishing the individual, has given most Americans more personal dignity and liberty than ever before. The individual freedoms destroyed by the increase in national authority have been in the main the freedom to deny black Americans their rights as citizens; the freedom to put small children to work in mills and immigrants in sweatshops; the freedom to pay starvation wages, require barbarous working hours, and permit squalid working conditions; the freedom to deceive in the sale of goods and securities; the freedom to pollute the environment—all freedoms that, one supposes, a civilized nation can readily do without.

"Statements are made," said President John F. Kennedy in 1963, "labelling the Federal Government an outsider, an intruder, an adversary. . . . The United States Government is not a stranger or not an enemy. It is the people of fifty states joining in a national effort. . . . Only a great national effort by a great people working together can explore the mysteries of space, harvest the products at the bottom of the ocean, and mobilize the human, natural, and material resources of our lands."

So an old debate continues. However, Americans are of two minds. When pollsters ask large, spacious questions—Do you think government has become too involved in your lives? Do you think government should stop regulating business?—a sizable majority opposes big government. But when asked specific questions about the practical work of government—Do you favor social security? unemployment compensation? Medicare? health and safety standards in factories? environmental protection? government guarantee of jobs for everyone seeking employment? price and wage controls when inflation threatens?—a sizable majority approves of intervention.

In general, Americans do not want less government. What they want is more efficient government. They want government to do a better job. For a time in the 1970s, with Vietnam and Watergate, Americans lost confidence in the national government. In 1964, more than three-quarters of those polled had thought the national government could be trusted to do right most of the time. By 1980 only one-quarter was prepared to offer such trust. But by 1984 trust in the federal government to manage national affairs had climbed back to 45 percent.

Bureaucracy is a term of abuse. But it is impossible to run any large organization, whether public or private, without a bureaucracy's division of labor and hierarchy of authority. And we live in a world of large organizations. Without bureaucracy modern society would collapse. The problem is not to abolish bureaucracy, but to make it flexible, efficient, and capable of innovation.

Two hundred years after the drafting of the Constitution, Americans still regard government with a mixture of reliance and mistrust—a good combination. Mistrust is the best way to keep government reliable. Informed criticism is the means of correcting governmental inefficiency, incompetence, and arbitrariness; that is, of best enabling government to play its essential role. For without government, we cannot attain the goals of the Founding Fathers. Without an understanding of government, we cannot have the informed criticism that makes government do the job right. It is the duty of every American citizen to know our government—which is what this series is all about.

In 1887, immigrants view the Statue of Liberty as they sail into New York harbor en route to the immigration inspection station at Ellis Island. The Statue of Liberty, originally called Liberty Enlightening the World, *has welcomed new arrivals to America's shores since 1886.*

ONE

A Nation of Immigrants

"Give me your tired, your poor, / your huddled masses yearning to breathe free." These words, from "The New Colossus," a poem by Emma Lazarus, adorn the base of the Statue of Liberty and have welcomed millions of immigrants who have sailed into New York harbor. Although the Statue of Liberty and the words carved into its base were not dedicated until 1886, they symbolize the ideals of freedom and opportunity that have motivated citizens of other nations to journey to the shores of the United States since the earliest days of the nation.

Immigrants arriving in New York City during the late 19th and early 20th centuries were inspected at Ellis Island, the country's major immigration-processing facility, located near the Statue of Liberty. Their dreams of a better life were interrupted by the harsh reality of inspection by immigration officials. Following signs that were printed in nine languages, the new arrivals entered the overcrowded maze of the registry room to await the poking and prodding of the health inspection required by U.S. immigration law. Medical examiners, who worked with immigration officials at entry points, checked first for obvious physical problems such as blindness, deafness, and lameness and then for contagious diseases such as leprosy or tuberculosis. Immigrants who had suspicious symptoms were marked "T.D."—meaning temporarily detained— with chalk and held at Ellis Island for further examination. If new arrivals were unable to satisfy the health requirements, they were put on a ship and returned to their homeland.

After the medical inspection, immigration officers interrogated newcomers about their destinations in America, their means of support, and their political beliefs. Suspected subversives (people who advocated the overthrow of the government) and criminals were marked "S.I."—meaning special inquiry—and held pending further investigation. The inspectors marked those who seemed incapable of supporting themselves "L.P.C."—meaning likely public charges (people who would be unable to support themselves and would rely on government funds to survive)—and they, too, were deported. For many of the 5,000 would-be immigrants who passed through Ellis Island each day, the inspection process was an unpleasant, confusing, and altogether overwhelming experience. But for those who made it through the inspections, the prospect of life in the United States was full of promise.

So many people endured the hardships of relocation because America was perceived as a land of freedom and opportunity. People from many different countries settled in the United States, and the country grew and prospered with the continuous influx of foreigners. Unlike most European nations, which are each populated primarily by one ethnic group, America became a melting pot—a mixture of the customs, cultures, and religions of many different nationalities and ethnic groups. The United States has benefited greatly from the contributions of immigrants such as Italian-born missionary Saint Frances Cabrini, German-born physicist Albert Einstein, and Cuban-born baseball player José Canseco.

For the first hundred years of its existence, the United States maintained an open-door immigration policy. Everyone who wanted to come to America was welcome. The country was huge, and there was ample space for all. But in the late 1800s, some Americans began to question the desirability of the open-door policy. The population stretched from the Atlantic to the Pacific, and land and job opportunities no longer seemed unlimited. Immigrants were coming in greater numbers than ever before—between 1880 and 1920 more than 23 million arrived, as opposed to only 4.5 million between 1830 and 1860. In addition, prejudices against certain ethnic groups raised fears that the country would be overrun by foreigners. Responding to calls to control the masses of immigrants, Congress began to enact legislation that restricted the flow of foreigners into America in the late 1800s. At the same time, Congress created a succession of agencies to administer the restrictions.

These agencies were the predecessors of today's Immigration and Naturalization Service (INS). The mission of the INS today is to administer and enforce the immigration and naturalization laws and policies set by Congress and the president. *Immigration* refers to the act of entering a country to

Frances Xavier Cabrini (1850–1917), known as "the saint of the immigrants," left Italy in 1880 to aid poor Italians in America. She established schools, orphanages, and hospitals in large cities throughout the United States. Mother Cabrini, who became a naturalized citizen in 1909, was the first U.S. citizen to be declared a saint by the Roman Catholic church.

17

A family crosses the U.S.-Mexico border illegally. Because of the annual limit on the number of immigrants admitted into the United States, many people try to enter the country without following the proper procedures. The INS is responsible for apprehending and expelling illegal aliens.

establish permanent residence. *Naturalization* is the official process by which people acquire citizenship in a country other than the nation of their birth.

The policies of immigration restriction remain in force, but current legislation provides a system of equitable numerical quotas that gives people from all nations an equal chance to migrate to the United States. However, the tremendous demand for entrance into the United States has not diminished. The number of applications for immigrant visas far exceeds the number available. (Visas are the official permits (stamped in a passport) that allow entrance into the United States and other countries.) Because immigration quotas prevent people from entering the country, more than a million now cross U.S. borders illegally each year.

Reconciling the American tradition of welcoming those whom George Washington called "the oppressed and the needy of the earth" with the realities of a nation committed to maintaining the quality of life for its existing population presents one of the major challenges facing the United States today. As the waiting lists for visas continue to lengthen and the number of illegal aliens entering each year increases, the INS endeavors to promote and protect the public health and safety, economic welfare, national security, and humanitarian interests of the United States now and in the years to come.

Upon landing on an island in the Bahamas, Christopher Columbus is greeted by the friendly Arawak, the native people whom he called Indians. Columbus's "discovery" in 1492 launched the exploration and colonization of the Americas by European nations.

TWO

Early Immigration to the United States

The news of Christopher Columbus's "discovery" of the Americas in 1492 set off a wave of exploration that sent scores of ships across the Atlantic. But the European explorers of the late 15th and early 16th centuries were not the first immigrants to the New World. Scientists believe that the first migration of people to North America occurred more than 30,000 years ago, during the last great Ice Age. The level of the Pacific Ocean was low enough to expose a land bridge from Asia to North America across what is now the Bering Strait (between Siberia and Alaska), making it possible for people to cross to the New World on foot. By 10,000 B.C., settlements had spread to the southernmost point of South America. These original immigrants were the ancestors of the native peoples who greeted Columbus (and whom Columbus mistakenly called Indians) and of present-day Native Americans.

The Colonial Period

The great European economic powers of the 1500s and 1600s—England, Spain, Portugal, the Netherlands, and France—colonized the Western Hemisphere to profit from its abundance of natural resources. The colonies were established primarily to supply raw materials to their parent countries, but they also strengthened the economies of the parent countries by consuming goods manufactured in Europe.

Some of the people who left Europe during the colonial period (1607–1775) hoped to find religious tolerance or political freedom in the New World, but most, responding to advertisements trumpeting the availability of land, sought to improve their economic opportunities. Many were extremely poor when they arrived.

Other people did not come to the colonies by choice. Criminals were shipped from English jails to America in the 1600s. In fact, England founded the state of Georgia as a penal colony for those who were unable to pay their debts. Also, from 1619 until Congress outlawed the international slave trade in 1807, several million black slaves were brought from Africa against their will.

The new territories in the Western Hemisphere became a smaller-scale version of Europe. This was especially true in North America, where the coastal English colonies were bordered on the south by Spanish settlements and on the north by French, with Dutch and Swedish colonies interspersed among the English colonies. However, the French and Indian War, fought by the British against the French (and their Indian allies) from 1754 to 1763, removed most of the French presence from Canada. The Dutch and Swedish settlements had been absorbed earlier into the English colonies of New York, New Jersey, Pennsylvania, and Delaware. Thus, by the mid-18th century, the English dominated what was soon to become the United States.

Throughout most of the colonial period, the goal of immigration policy was the recruitment of labor. The English Parliament and local colonial governments sought to increase the flow of immigrants through land grants, employment incentives, and transportation payments. Advertisements heralding the availability of land and guaranteeing rights, freedoms, and religious tolerance appeared in Europe to attract workers. Most significantly, the practice of indentured service was widespread in the American colonies. An *indentured servant* was a person who bound himself or herself to work for another person for a specified time (usually for four to seven years) in return for payment of travel and living expenses. Upon fulfilling their contracts, former indentured servants usually received clothing, a gun, and land, and they were readily accepted into the community.

The colonists of English descent held varying attitudes toward the immigrants of other ethnic groups. For instance, early settlers from western Germany had been attracted to America by the advertisements of William Penn, the Englishman to whom King Charles II in 1681 had granted the land that became Pennsylvania. The Germans, who were excellent farmers, helped the local economy to flourish. They also shared the Protestant religious beliefs of the English and were admired for their good morals and work habits.

In 1681, William Penn (1644–1718), a prominent English Quaker and re-former, received the territory that became Pennsylvania from King Charles II as payment for a debt. Penn, who had been jailed in England for his reli-gious writings, established Pennsylvania as a sanctuary of religious freedom and democracy.

However, some colonists questioned whether the Germans—with their different background, language, and customs—would ever truly assimilate into a society dominated by Anglo-Americans and whether their presence benefited or harmed the country. Concerns about the assimilation of immigrants from different cultures would become an important issue in the history of the United States, one that would be debated repeatedly as each wave of immigrants landed on American shores. The evolution of United States immigration policy reflects changing attitudes toward different ethnic groups, as well as changing conditions in economic opportunity, population, and national security.

The Open-Door Era

The skepticism toward "foreigners" (non-English settlers) that began to emerge in the colonial period was overridden by the immediate concerns of the new nation. In 1776, when Thomas Jefferson stated the offenses of King

The Moravian village of Bethlehem, Pennsylvania. During the 1700s, many ethnic and religious groups—including Moravians, Mennonites, and Amish— migrated to the British colonies. These groups often established separate villages to avoid English-speaking colonists.

George III against the American colonies in the Declaration of Independence, high on his list was the monarch's refusal to grant the colonists' demand for a more liberal immigration policy. "He has endeavored to prevent the population of these states"; Jefferson wrote, "for that purpose obstructing the laws of naturalization of foreigners; [and] refusing to pass others to encourage their migrations hither." Jefferson and his compatriots in the Second Continental Congress realized that immigration had been important to the growth of the colonies and that it would be important to the new nation's future.

After the American Revolution, the doors of the country were opened to all peoples for a variety of practical and ideological reasons. The land was rich and expansive, but there were relatively few inhabitants. From 1630 to 1790, well under a million people had immigrated to the area that became the United States. When the first census was taken in 1790, the total population of the United States was 3,227,000. The population density was about 4.5 people per square mile (compared to 64 per square mile as of the 1980 census). For the country to continue to grow and prosper, a vast amount of labor was needed to form communities, to clear farmland, and to push back the frontier. People were also needed to protect the country in case of another war—to ensure that the United States would never be conquered by a foreign power. In addition, most early Americans firmly believed that their new nation was founded on the principles of freedom and democracy set forth in the Declaration of Independence and that all people should be welcome, regardless of their national origin.

The Constitution does not contain specific provisions for regulating immigration and naturalization, except regarding the slave trade. (Article 1, Section 9 states: "The Migration or Importation of such persons as any of the States now existing shall think proper to admit shall not be prohibited by the Congress prior to the Year one thousand eight hundred and eight.") The framers of the document intended that Congress establish and amend immigration policy. In 1790, one year after the Constitution was ratified by the states, Congress passed the first Naturalization Act, which established a liberal policy for granting citizenship. Any free white person could become a citizen by residing in the United States for two years and renouncing all allegiances to foreign sovereigns. Opponents of the measure argued for stricter naturalization

President John Adams, a Federalist, signed the anti-immigrant Alien and Sedition Acts in 1798. Because most immigrants supported the rival Democratic-Republican party, the legislation—which the Federalist Congress set to expire after the 1800 presidential election—was interpreted as a means to harass immigrants and deny them the right to vote.

requirements and for regulations prohibiting the admission of paupers, vagrants, and the outcasts of Europe (a phrase used during the congressional debate). By 1795, the turmoil in Europe caused by the French Revolution (1789–99) had increased fears of foreign political influence in the United States. Some Americans believed that if many dangerous foreign radicals were allowed to enter the country, they might attempt to overthrow the government. Consequently, the Naturalization Act of 1795 was more stringent than its predecessor, requiring a five-year period of residency and renunciation of all allegiances and titles of nobility.

This particular episode of xenophobia (a distrust and fear of foreigners) reached its peak during an undeclared naval war between France and the United States. In 1798, France seized more than 300 U.S. merchant ships in response to the United States's apparent support of England's war effort against the revolutionary government of France. During the next two years, the U.S. Navy, in reprisal for the seizures, captured or sank 84 French warships. President John Adams used the emotion of the times to the political advantage of his party, the Federalists. Because most incoming foreigners supported the rival Democratic-Republican party of Thomas Jefferson, Adams hoped to restrict immigration and thus decrease the numbers and power of his opposition. In 1798, Congress passed four laws that were collectively known as the Alien and Sedition Acts:

- A stricter Naturalization Act required 14 years of residency to obtain citizenship.
- The Act Respecting Alien Enemies gave the president the power to deport (the legal expulsion of an alien from the country) all alien enemies in the event of war.
- The Act Concerning Aliens gave the president power to deport any alien whom he considered a threat to the nation's peace and security whether a state of war existed or not.
- The Act for the Punishment of Certain Crimes (Sedition Act) made it a crime to criticize the government or its officials.

Because the president—Adams at that time—was the sole arbiter of who constituted a threat, the Jeffersonians were outraged at the passage of the Alien and Sedition Acts. Although Adams never used the authority granted to him to deport anyone, 25 people were jailed for criticizing the president.

When Jefferson became president in 1801, the antialien fervor subsided somewhat because tensions with France had diminished. The alien acts were

Immigrants dance below deck en route to the United States in 1856. Immigrants usually purchased tickets for passage in the steerage section of the ship, where fares were the lowest.

allowed to expire, and a new naturalization act reestablishing the five-year residency period of the 1795 act was passed in 1802. This was the only federal act regulating immigration and naturalization for almost 75 years. State and local governments exercised authority over immigration until after the Civil War. Many coastal states established immigration boards that were operated by social reformers and humanitarians. Their enforcement procedures tended to be informal and lax.

During the first half of the 19th century, the federal government did little to supervise or control immigration. Congress did pass steerage legislation in 1819. Steerage was the section of the ship often reserved for the poorest passengers, and this law established minimum standards—such as the maximum number of passengers—for the treatment of travelers in steerage. Congress intended to stimulate immigration by providing safer transportation, but the increased cost of passage made it more difficult for prospective immigrants to come to America. The legislation also provided means to count immigrants entering the country by requiring all ship captains landing at Atlantic ports and New Orleans to furnish the collector of customs with lists of passengers. An amendment in 1850 required passenger lists for ships landing on the West Coast.

In the 50 years between the end of the revolution and 1830, about 375,000 immigrants had come to the United States. For the most part, they were from England and the countries of northwestern Europe, such as Germany, the Netherlands, Norway, Sweden, and Denmark. These groups were generally welcomed, as the German settlers of Pennsylvania had been. But between 1830 and 1860, the number of immigrants coming to the United States increased dramatically. Almost 4,500,000 Europeans crossed the Atlantic during this 30-year period. In the 1840s, a plant disease—late potato blight—destroyed Ireland's potato crop. Because potatoes were that country's staple crop, its main source of food, the resulting potato famines compelled millions of Irish to leave their native country for the United States. Economic depressions in Germany had similar effects. Many Germans lost their jobs and turned to America for opportunity.

A significant factor distinguished the people in this wave of immigration from earlier ones. For the most part, the immigrants who came during the first 50 years of the Republic practiced the same form of Christianity—Protestantism— as the Anglo-Americans who made up the vast majority of the United States population. But the Irish and southern Germans who arrived during the middle of the 19th century were for the most part Roman Catholic, and there were also a number of Jews from Germany.

Religion was very important to Americans during this period, and the historical animosity between Protestants and Catholics caused a great deal of friction between many Anglo-Americans and the new immigrant groups. The conflict had its roots in the centuries-old religious and political struggles of Europe, which were particularly evident in the British Isles. (A similar hatred between Protestants and Catholics can be seen today in the violent confrontations in Northern Ireland.) Thus 19th-century Americans of English descent held a deep-seated prejudice toward the beliefs of the incoming Irish and German Catholics. They did not want the religious battles that had raged in Europe to destroy their country. Some of the earliest Americans, the Puritans who settled New England, had come to the country seeking religious freedom. Their descendants were suspicious of those whose actions, at least as they saw it, were controlled by a pope. Many American Protestants were genuinely afraid that the pope was trying to extend his authority over them by colonizing their country with Catholics.

Many of the new immigrants were very poor and lived in squalor in the large cities of the East. They were widely accused of vagrancy and criminal activity. Irish and German immigrants were scorned by some for their purported love of whiskey and beer. Although the moderate consumption of alcohol was generally accepted during the 18th century, in the 19th century temperance groups, which advocated abstinence from alcohol and lobbied for laws prohibiting the production, sale, and consumption of alcohol, sprang up throughout the country. In addition, newcomers encountered hostility from labor groups. Because they were poor, immigrants would work for very low wages, which meant that native workers were forced to accept lower wages in order to compete for job opportunities. Not surprisingly, businesspeople who employed large labor forces favored immigration for this very reason.

The negative feelings toward immigrants during this era gave rise to a movement known as nativism. Because they feared that America might be taken over by foreigners with subversive intentions, nativists were eager to restrict immigration severely and to eliminate the participation of foreigners in the political affairs of the country. They wanted to preserve the ethnic purity

Paddy's Ladder to Wealth in a Free Country.

Irish immigrants flooded U.S. cities to escape the hunger and poverty caused by the potato famines that devastated Ireland in the mid-19th century. They were often caricatured by cartoonists as "Paddys" (a derogatory term for Irish immigrants), with apelike features such as a jutting jaw and a sloping forehead.

of the country's Anglo-Saxon heritage and to uphold what they considered to be the moral superiority of Protestantism over Catholicism. One of their most popular slogans in the 1840s and 1850s was, Our Country, Our Whole Country, and Nothing But Our Country. To this end, the nativists formed associations, such as the Sons of the Sires of '76 and the American Brotherhood, to present their views and to agitate for reform of immigration and naturalization policy.

The culmination of the political activities of these organizations was the Know-Nothing party, also known as the Native American party, which became an important force in the 1850s. The party's origins can be traced to the most noteworthy of the nativist societies, the Supreme Order of the Star-Spangled Banner, a group founded in the state of New York in 1850. The organization had a national council, plus state and local chapters. To become a member, one had to be descended from at least two generations of American ancestors, and no family members or ancestors could have been members of the Roman Catholic church for two generations. The organization was originally a secret society. Whenever members were asked about its activities, they would reply "I know nothing," which is how the party got its name.

Because the Know-Nothings hoped to limit immigration and keep foreigners from participating in politics, their goal was to elect to office only native Americans who agreed with the party's aims and could help bring about the reforms they desired. The success of Know-Nothing candidates in the elections of the 1850s was fairly widespread. In 1854, Massachusetts elected a Know-Nothing governor, Pennsylvania elected a governor with ties to the party, and the citizens of New York elected 40 Know-Nothings to its state legislature. The next year, six states—including New Hampshire, Connecticut, and California—elected Know-Nothing governors, and many states sent members of the party to serve in Congress.

However, these victories by candidates of the Know-Nothing party were not necessarily victories for the cause of nativism. In fact, the changing political atmosphere of the 1850s contributed as much to the Know-Nothing victories as did the electorate's fear of immigrants. The two major parties of the previous decade were the Democrats and the Whigs, but the influence of the Whigs had begun to deteriorate in the early years of the 1850s. Many members of that party had become disenchanted with the bickering over the issue of slavery and with the party's lack of effective leadership. They would not vote for their traditional enemies, the Democrats, so they turned to the only alternative, the Know-Nothings. The successes of the Know-Nothing party in 1854 and 1855 were short-lived, primarily because a more attractive alternative for the former Whigs quickly appeared on the political scene—the newly created Republican

A Know-Nothing meeting in New York City in 1855. The Know-Nothing party, officially known as the Native American party, was an anti-immigrant, anti-Catholic political organization that flourished during the 1850s. The party advocated increasing the naturalization period from 5 to 21 years and excluding Catholics and immigrants from holding public office.

party (which should not be confused with the Democratic-Republican party of Thomas Jefferson in the early years of the century). Democrat James Buchanan won the presidential election of 1856, and Republican John C. Frémont finished a strong second. Former President Millard Fillmore, the Know-Nothing candidate, ran a distant third, signaling the end of the Know-Nothings as an important political movement.

Although the Know-Nothings succeeded in getting a few of their candidates into office briefly, they fell far short of achieving their goals. The victories of the party in certain regions, such as the eastern cities, perhaps reflected an intense xenophobia on the part of a small but vocal portion of the population, but immigration and naturalization policy remained unchanged on the national level. The continued demand for labor to help the country expand across the

31

RIOT AT HOBOKEN.

An 1851 riot in Hoboken, New Jersey, between Germans celebrating May Day and a gang of New York City rowdies known as the Short Boys. Catholic immigrants from Germany and Ireland were frequent victims of violence because their religious beliefs differed from the Protestantism practiced by many Americans.

North American continent, as well as the traditional American ideals of freedom and opportunity, kept the gates of the country open to all who wanted to enter.

Perhaps more significant than the election of Know-Nothing candidates during this period was the violence inspired by nativist fears. In the 1840s, the Roman Catholic bishop Francis Patrick Kenrick of Philadelphia wrote a letter to the city school authorities complaining about the practice of reading the Protestant version of the Bible in class. He asked that Roman Catholics be allowed to read their own Bible and that they be exempted from all religious instruction. When the city granted the request, Protestants became enraged and began passing out pamphlets that described the Catholic plot to "kick the Bible out of the schools." In May 1844, tensions became so strained in the predominantly Irish suburb of Kensington that a riot erupted, lasting several days. Several people were killed, St. Michael's and St. Anthony's churches were burned, and Catholic schools were vandalized. The crew of the USS *Princeton* had to be landed in order to restore order.

Other incidents of violence against Catholics were common. In 1854, Gaetano Bedini, a representative of Pope Pius IX, visited the United States to settle a dispute over church property in Buffalo, New York. His subsequent tour of cities around the country was greeted everywhere by angry mobs of anti-Catholic nativists. In separate incidents, the Ursuline Convent in Charlestown, Massachusetts, was burned to the ground, services at churches in Maine were interrupted by the tossing of rotten eggs, and windows of Catholic churches around Boston were broken regularly. Anti-Catholic propaganda, which was churned out in abundance by groups who hoped to discredit the immigrant population, helped to increase tensions in the cities and to incite these acts of terror.

The controversy caused by the growing tide of immigrants arriving in the United States during the middle of the 1800s was only a prelude to the furor that would rage at the end of that century and the beginning of the next. Although the nativists made no concrete institutional gains during this period, the anti-immigrant movement was gathering momentum as an American social force. As the influx of new arrivals increased, policymakers began to realize that the federal government must devote more attention to immigration issues. It would be only 50 years before Abraham Lincoln's fear—that nativists would rewrite the Declaration of Independence to read, "All men are created equal, except Negroes, and foreigners, and Catholics"—would be reflected in official immigration policy.

An eye examination at Ellis Island in 1913. After arriving at Ellis Island, immigrants made their way through an assembly line of doctors, each looking for a specific disease. Those who passed the health inspection were interviewed by immigration officers to determine whether they should otherwise be barred from entering the country for any other reason, such as having a criminal record or lacking employable skills.

THREE

The Need for Regulation

In spite of the political agitation of the nativists and the violence directed at immigrants, the federal government maintained an open-door policy toward immigration during the mid-19th century. During this period, the Republican party endorsed a generous federal immigration policy. Its 1864 platform asserted: "Foreign immigration which in the past has added so much to the wealth, resources, and increase of power to this nation—the asylum of the oppressed of all nations—should be fostered and encouraged by a liberal and just policy." In the same year, President Abraham Lincoln signed an act that established within the State Department a Bureau of Immigration to promote immigration to America in the years immediately following the Civil War. Four years of war had greatly depleted the nation's work force, and Lincoln concluded that it was necessary to recruit labor abroad in order to restore productivity. The Bureau of Immigration sent agents to Europe to find workers interested in coming to the United States. The bureau had a brief life, however, lasting only until 1868, when the government decided that the immediate shortage was over. Nevertheless, a strong demand for labor still existed. The United States was expanding west across the continent. Thousands of workers were needed to lay tracks for the railroads, and settlers were needed to farm the fertile land of the prairies. In urban areas, textile mills, meat-packing plants, and other emerging industries required many unskilled workers. Opportunities were abundant, and immigrants kept coming to America to build a better life.

In contrast to the federal government, several city and state governments enacted legislation in an effort to control the massive influx of immigrants. The millions of newcomers caused significant problems in the major port cities. Many of the immigrants were sick or very poor, and they often became public charges. Providing for immigrants was costly, and, even in the early 19th century, some local governments passed laws to prevent unfit and unproductive new arrivals from joining their communities.

In 1824, New York City enacted the nation's first local immigration law. It required all immigrants who intended to stay in the city to report to the mayor's office or the city magistrate within 24 hours of their arrival. In addition, the statute required all ship captains to furnish a $300 bond of indemnity against the expenses caused by aliens brought in and not reported. A bond of indemnity—similar to an insurance policy—paid the city if public funds had to be used for supporting immigrants. In 1833, Baltimore began requiring captains to pay a tax of $1.50 for each immigrant or to provide a bond of $150 good for 2 years. Massachusetts passed a law in 1837 requiring the inspection of all arriving

The U.S. Army recruits immigrants in front of Castle Garden in the 19th century. Castle Garden, located at the southern tip of Manhattan, served as New York City's immigrant reception center until 1890, when the federal government assumed sole responsibility for inspecting immigrants.

aliens. No "lunatics," "idiots," paupers, maimed, aged, or infirm persons unable to support themselves could be landed unless the captain provided a $1,000 bond good for 10 years. The state also imposed a tax of two dollars per immigrant.

To cope with the ever-increasing number of immigrants arriving in New York City, local immigration officials established a facility to inspect incoming foreigners. Converted from a former theater, Castle Garden served as the principal immigration station of New York City (and the nation) from 1855 to 1890. Castle Garden contained a hospital, bathing facilities, and a communal kitchen, and its all-volunteer staff provided practical advice, medical examinations, and other social services to newcomers.

Other regions of the country later adopted immigration laws similar to the legislation enacted on the East Coast. In 1869, Louisiana passed a law that excluded foreigners likely to become public charges unless bonds were provided. California established a law in 1870 to prevent the importation of Asian prostitutes by prohibiting the entry of Chinese, Mongolian, and Japanese females who could not prove that they were immigrating voluntarily and that they were of decent character. The law was soon extended to males in order to decrease the flow of Asian contract workers. These laws coincided with the increasing number of Chinese laborers who had come to the American West to build the railroads or work in the mines. By 1869, 63,000 Chinese had come to the United States, and twice that number arrived during the 1870s. In the Burlingame Treaty of 1868 between the United States and China, the U.S. government had guaranteed that it would not impede the flow of Chinese workers entering the country. But, like the Irish and German immigrants in the previous decades, Asians were victims of harsh—and at times violent— xenophobia. During riots in Los Angeles in 1871, 15 Chinese were lynched, and 6 were shot. Gangs of nativist hoodlums destroyed the homes of Chinese immigrants during riots in San Francisco in 1877, which culminated that summer in the burning of 25 Chinese laundries.

The federal government finally followed the regulatory lead set by local jurisdictions by adopting the first national immigration act in 1875. The statute merely banned the entry of convicts and prostitutes. A more important event in the development of American immigration law occurred the following year when the Supreme Court struck down all state legislation regulating immigration. In *Henderson v. Mayor of New York*, the Court ruled that state immigration laws, which required bonds and head taxes (charges for entering the country), were unconstitutional because they encroached upon the exclusive power vested in Congress to regulate interstate and foreign commerce, as

Chinese railroad workers in the Sierra Nevada mountains in 1887. The Central Pacific Railroad Company recruited Chinese laborers to lay the track for the transcontinental railroad. The Chinese Exclusion Act of 1882, which Congress passed in response to the public outcry on the West Coast against the influx of Chinese workers, produced a dramatic drop in the number of legal Chinese immigrants— from 40,000 in 1881 to 10 in 1887.

provided by Article 1, Section 8, of the Constitution. This landmark decision set the stage for the federal government to assume direct control of immigration policy.

The number of immigrants entering the United States was increasing dramatically, from 143,000 in the decade between 1820 and 1830 to more than 2.8 million between 1870 and 1880. But in the 1880s, a second surge of mass immigration from Europe, similar to the one that occurred between 1830 and 1860, began. The new immigrants were not from northern and western Europe. Steam-powered ships had reduced the time required to cross the Atlantic to 10 days (wind-driven ships had taken 1 to 3 months). Passenger lines began operating from southern Europe, and immigration was no longer tied to America's trading partners in northern and western Europe. The newcomers were predominantly Italian or Jewish peasants from southern and eastern Europe.

Americans who were skeptical of immigrants again questioned whether these peoples would be able to assimilate into the culture of the United States and whether they would be worthy and productive citizens. Nativists, hoping to keep out "undesirable" immigrants, launched a new drive for restrictive legislation. They publicized theories, widely believed at the time, that eastern and southern Europeans were biologically inferior to the traditional Anglo-Saxon stock. In the early 1900s, University of Wisconsin sociology professor Edward A. Ross, a leading nativist, asserted that Italians possessed "a distressing frequency of low foreheads, open mouths, weak chins, [and] poor features" and lacked "the rational power to take care of themselves." He claimed that Jews were undersized and extremely sensitive to pain, remarking that it would be impossible to make Boy Scouts of them. In his popular book *Passing of the Great Races,* New York zoologist Madison Grant argued that the newcomers "contained a large number of the weak, the broken, and the mentally crippled of all races drawn from the lowest stratum of the Mediterranean basin and the Balkans, along with hordes of the wretched, submerged populations of the Polish ghettos." Chinese, Jews, and Italians were also said to have extreme criminal tendencies. Theodore Bingham, police commissioner of New York City (1906–9), said that 85 percent of that city's criminals were of foreign origin. Furthermore, many Protestant Americans were prejudiced

The descendants of 19th-century immigrants crowd around the stalwart "last Yankee," predicted by an 1888 cartoonist to be a rarity in the 20th century. In the late 19th and early 20th centuries, many Americans feared that unrestricted immigration would harm the biological and cultural stock of the country and called for the enactment of legislation to limit immigration.

AND WE OPEN OUR ARMS TO THEM!

An 1883 cartoon appearing in Life *magazine shows European rulers sweeping outcasts from their country into the United States. Many people believed that the United States could no longer sustain large numbers of immigrants, especially those lacking education or employable skills.*

against Jews and Italian Catholics on religious grounds. The nativists argued that the unrestricted flood of new immigrants would destroy the ethnic purity and moral fabric of American society.

The nativism that emerged earlier in the century had been neutralized by a general belief that America should uphold its tradition of welcoming those in need and that there was ample room for everyone who wanted to come. However, the second wave of immigration was much larger than the first. Between 1880 and 1920, more than 23 million foreigners entered the United States, compared with 4.5 million during the period from 1830 to 1860. Several factors led to the change in public attitude toward immigration. The American frontier was virtually closed by the end of the century. Farmland was less plentiful, and industrial cities were growing increasingly crowded. Several financial panics during the 1890s convinced many that the United States could no longer support the large number of immigrants. Finally, technological advances such as mechanical reapers, sewing machines, and electric motors greatly reduced the need for the unskilled labor of immigrants. People began to worry that there was no longer enough room for newcomers, and immigration became an important and volatile issue.

The Era of Regulation

In the late 19th century, Congress, reacting to calls for restrictions on immigration, enacted a series of laws that prevented the entry of foreigners deemed undesirable. During this period, the bureaucracy that would manage the new federal immigration policy (the forerunner of the modern INS) began to develop.

In 1875, Congress enacted an immigration statute that prohibited the entry of convicts and prostitutes, and in 1882 it passed the first comprehensive federal immigration law. The Immigration Act of 1882—reminiscent of the 1837 Massachusetts law—banned "lunatics," "idiots," and those likely to become public charges from entering the country. The 1882 act delegated authority to the secretary of the Treasury to administer and enforce immigration policy. The Treasury Department used Customs Service personnel, who were already inspecting cargo at U.S. ports, and hired state immigration boards and agencies to inspect all arriving immigrants to determine whether they fell into one of the excluded groups—convicts, lunatics, idiots, etc. Congress established a head tax of 50 cents, paid by each immigrant, to finance the inspection program and to care for needy immigrants.

Massachusetts historian and statesman Henry Cabot Lodge was an outspoken advocate of immigration restriction. Lodge served in the House of Representatives (1887–93) and in the Senate (1893–1924), where he was one of the leading supporters of the Immigration Act of 1917.

A Chinese immigrant hangs on to the tree of liberty as Republicans and Democrats pass the Chinese Exclusion Act of 1882, which prohibited the entry of Chinese immigrants for 10 years. Although some Americans felt that the wholesale exclusion of Chinese immigrants violated the American ideal of liberty and freedom to all, Congress maintained the ban on Chinese immigration until 1943.

One of the leading proponents of the 1882 bill was historian Henry Cabot Lodge, who argued that the "great Republic should no longer be left unguarded" from the waves of Italians and Jews. Lodge and his allies were known as *restrictionists* because they wanted to limit severely the numbers of foreigners allowed to enter the United States.

On the West Coast, anti-Chinese sentiment had continued to mount throughout the 1870s. Labor organizations lobbied for restrictions on the immigration of Chinese workers, who were competing with native laborers for jobs. A new treaty with China permitted the United States to regulate, limit, or suspend but not absolutely prohibit the immigration of Chinese laborers. Congress took advantage of the provision to pass the Chinese Exclusion Act of 1882. The act barred the entry of all Chinese laborers into the United States for a period of 10 years and prohibited federal and state courts from granting citizenship to Chinese immigrants. A loophole in the law allowed the entry of wealthy Chinese merchants and students, and any Chinese who had been in the country before the ban could become a naturalized citizen. Since immigration legislation allowed foreign-born children of U.S. citizens to immigrate, many Chinese became "paper sons"—people who were not really children of Chinese Americans but who purchased forged birth certificates in order to enter the country. However, officials at Angel Island, the immigration-processing center located in San Francisco Bay, rigorously interrogated and detained Chinese people claiming to have American parents, and many paper sons were subsequently deported. Congress extended the Chinese Exclusion Act another 10 years in 1892 and indefinitely in 1902. It was not repealed until 1943.

In the late 19th century leaders of organized labor, such as Samuel Gompers of the American Federation of Labor and John Mitchell of the United Mine Workers, also spoke out against immigrants. They claimed that the influx of cheap foreign labor took jobs away from American workers. Employers often recruited and paid the transportation costs for large numbers of foreign workers—called *contract workers* because they signed a contract to work for a specific period of time—because they could pay foreign workers less than American workers. Labor leaders were instrumental in lobbying Congress for the passage of the Foran Act (1885), which prohibited employers from importing alien contract laborers. Only skilled workers—such as engineers, nurses, and carpenters—and teachers were exempted. Restrictionists hoped that the limitations on immigration imposed during the 1880s would be extended, and many Americans supported the drive for tougher legislation. The anti-Catholic American Protective Association was formed in 1887, and prominent New Englanders established the first Immigration Restriction League in Boston in 1894. These groups, like the earlier Know-Nothing organizations of the 1850s, led the fight to exclude supposedly inferior and undesirable aliens. Although the activities of the earlier nativist groups had little effect on government policy, the more clamorous calls for immigration restriction at the end of the 19th century succeeded.

Immigrants arrive in New York City in 1882 to replace striking American workers. Labor unions objected to contract workers—immigrants whose passage was prepaid by employers—because they were willing to work for lower wages than were American laborers.

In 1891, Congress established within the Treasury Department a permanent superintendent of immigration to supervise and administer federal immigration policy. President Benjamin Harrison appointed William D. Owen, a former congressman from Indiana, to the post of superintendent on July 1 of that year. Congress also increased the list of inadmissible aliens to include polygamists (people married to more than one person) and those with "loathsome and contagious diseases." In order to determine which immigrants were sick, the statute required that all arriving aliens receive a thorough medical examination performed by officers of the Marine Hospital Service (the predecessor of the Public Health Service). In addition, all aliens who became public charges after one year could be deported. Finally, the statute established for the first time immigration inspectors along the land borders of the United States, and it established 22 Canadian and 2 Mexican border stations. These inspectors were the forerunners of INS inspectors now stationed at border stations and other points of entry.

44

When Castle Garden closed down in 1890, immigration officials inspected arrivals landing in New York at the Barge Office on the Manhattan docks until the facilities at Ellis Island were built. Ellis Island opened in 1892, becoming the nation's main immigrant-processing facility.

To help cope with the growing number of immigrants and to administer the nation's immigration policy more efficiently, Congress expanded the bureaucratic structure for immigration enforcement by creating a new Bureau of Immigration in 1903. Because immigration was now viewed as a factor that affected the supply and demand of labor and wages, Congress transferred the bureau from the Treasury Department to the newly created Department of Commerce and Labor. Further amendments to the Immigration Act that year banned the entrance of epileptics, beggars, white slavers (people who imported females expressly for prostitution), and anarchists (people who believe in the elimination of all governmental control over individuals). The inclusion of the last category resulted from the assassination of President William McKinley in 1901 by Leon Czolgosz, an anarchist whose parents were Polish immigrants.

The next major change in United States immigration policy came in 1906, when Congress enacted the first naturalization law in more than 100 years.

Ellis Island, a 27.5-acre island off the New Jersey shoreline in Upper New York harbor, was the country's major immigrant-inspection station from 1892 to 1924.

Ellis Island— Gateway to America

Ellis Island, located near the Statue of Liberty in Upper New York Bay, served as the primary immigration station for the United States from 1892 to 1924. During that period, 12 million immigrants (75 percent of the national total) passed through the island's immigration station.

Ellis Island—known by many names before it was purchased by Samuel Ellis, a butcher, in the 1770s—was once used by Dutch settlers as a picnic ground and by later colonists as a site for hanging traitors and pirates. The state of New York later acquired the island to enhance its harbor defense. In 1808, the U.S. government bought the island for $10,000 to use as an arsenal and fort.

The federal government assumed full responsibility for the reception of immigrants in 1890. In April of that year, Congress appropriated $75,000 to the Treasury Department for the establishment of an immigration station for the Port of New York on Ellis Island.

On January 1, 1892, the Ellis Island immigration station opened to process steerage passengers. (First- and second-class passengers were processed on board ship and disembarked directly in Manhattan.) The depot, built at the cost of $500,000, contained a large 2-story processing building, separate hospital and laundry facilities, and dormitories for detainees.

Many of the island's buildings were destroyed by a fire in 1897. No lives were lost, but most of the immigration records dating from 1855 were destroyed. A new, fireproof facility—designed to meet the needs of 500,000 immigrants each year (the annual number of arrivals expected by immigration officials) and constructed at a cost of $1.5 million—opened in December 1900. The impressive French Renaissance–style brick structure contained a large examination hall, administrative offices, two dormitories for detainees, telegraph and railroad offices, a baggage room, and kitchen, laundry, and bathing facilities.

In 1902, President Theodore Roosevelt "cleaned house" at Ellis Island following scandals that exposed graft and brutality by immigration officials. Roosevelt named William Williams, a respected young Wall Street attorney, as the new commissioner of immigration for the Port of New York, and he made changes to ensure the efficient, honest, courteous, and sanitary treatment of immigrants. As early as 1903, however, Ellis Island was bulging at the seams. Despite the addition of new buildings, the island's facilities lagged behind the demands placed upon them by the massive numbers of immigrants passing through the station. At the height of its activity, Ellis Island processed more than a million people annually—twice its intended capacity.

During World War I, Ellis Island was used as a military hospital and as a detention center for suspected enemy aliens. After the war, immigration resumed at prewar levels, and Congress passed the Immigration Act of 1921 to reduce the number of immigrants entering the United States. The act set an annual limit of 355,000 European immigrants and established a quota system based on national origins. Nonetheless, Ellis Island remained overcrowded as steamship companies rushed to deliver their passengers before each month's quota was depleted. Several commissioners of immigration at Ellis Island resigned in frustration because their requests for renovations were ignored.

In 1924, when the examination of aliens began to be conducted in immigrants' countries of origin, Ellis Island was transformed from the nation's primary immigrant inspection station to a center for the detention and deportation of aliens who had entered the United States illegally or who had violated the terms of their visas. As Ellis Island lodged fewer and fewer aliens, its buildings slowly fell into disrepair. As a result of the liberal detention policy established by the Immigration and Naturalization Act of 1952, the number of detainees fell to fewer than 30 in 1954. The Ellis Island facility, con-

The examination hall of the Ellis Island immigration station in 1904.

sisting of 40 structures on 27.5 acres, was closed in November 1954. On May 11, 1965, President Lyndon B. Johnson declared Ellis Island part of the Statue of Liberty National Monument, thus placing the island under the jurisdiction of the National Park Service.

Restoration work on the northern part of Ellis Island—funded by $150 million in private donations—began in 1984. The main registry building, which will contain the Ellis Island Immigration Museum, will open to the public in late 1990, and the entire project is scheduled for completion in time for the Ellis Island centennial celebration in 1992.

President Theodore Roosevelt had appointed a special commission the previous year to study the problems of the naturalization process, and the commission's findings prompted changes in the law. Before the new legislation, the executive branch of the federal government had no administrative control over the naturalization process, which was performed by federal courts and certain state courts. The lack of centralized control meant that naturalization practices were not standardized. Some courts paid attention to the requirements of the law, making sure that applicants had fulfilled the necessary five-year residency period and that they were of good character. Other courts, however, were not so strict, and naturalization fraud became widespread by the early 1900s. It was common for big-city political bosses to herd large groups of immigrants into naturalization courtrooms on the eve of an election.

Congress passed the Naturalization Act of 1906 to prevent inconsistencies and abuses by establishing federal administrative supervision over the naturalization process. Federal courts still conducted naturalization ceremonies, but the paperwork and investigative procedures were centralized. The bureau stationed 300 naturalization examiners in 23 districts throughout the country to ensure that the procedures and standards for naturalization would be closely followed.

The Naturalization Act established a procedure for attaining citizenship that basically remains in force today. An alien applying for citizenship must

- File a declaration of intention that he or she wants to become a citizen (known as first papers, but not required since 1952).
- File a petition for naturalization (second papers).
- Appear for a court hearing on the petition, by which the certificate of naturalized citizenship (final papers) will be granted or denied.

At the naturalization hearing, the applicant is required to prove continuous residence in the United States for at least five years, to produce two witnesses who will attest to the applicant's good moral character and attachment to the principles of the Constitution, to demonstrate a basic knowledge of American history and civics, and to show that he or she can speak English. If the applicant fulfills these requirements, the judge will administer the oath of allegiance, and the person becomes a naturalized U.S. citizen.

The 1906 act also changed the Bureau of Immigration to the Bureau of Immigration and Naturalization, bringing naturalization under the jurisdiction of a commissioner general of immigration. President Roosevelt appointed Frank Sargent, a former grand master of the Brotherhood of Locomotive Firemen, to

Frank Sargent, commissioner general of immigration (1902–8), initiated procedures to bar criminals and other undesirable aliens from immigrating and instituted methods to prevent fraud from being committed against immigrants. Sargent also concentrated on preventing the smuggling of Chinese across the Mexican and Canadian borders.

the post in 1902 (where he served until his death in 1908). As a proponent of organized labor, Sargent was one of the leaders in tightening immigration restriction during the early years of the 20th century. Sargent recommended more categories for exclusion, including "moral perverts" and those over 60 years old or under 17 traveling alone unless they had relatives in the United States able to provide for them. He also insisted that U.S. land borders were inadequately guarded.

Despite the constant tightening of immigration law that had taken place since the 1880s, restrictionists remained dissatisfied with the efforts of the government to stop the flow of "inferior" immigrants. They continued to agitate for additional limitations, hoping to eliminate completely the entry of southern and eastern Europeans. In order to achieve their goals without appearing to be openly prejudiced against certain nationalities and races, restrictionists began advocating a particularly treacherous barrier to immigration: the literacy test. The purported object of the literacy test was to ensure that all male adult immigrants could read and write their native language. The restrictionists knew that most immigrants were very poor, had received little education, and would be turned away because they would not be able to meet the literacy requirement. Better-educated immigrants from England and Scandinavia, whom the restrictionists considered desirable, would be able to pass the test and would be allowed to enter. In 1895, Henry Cabot Lodge, by then a U.S. senator, introduced the first immigration bill containing a literacy requirement, and it passed both houses of Congress. President Grover Cleveland vetoed the bill, however, saying that it conflicted with the principles of freedom and opportunity upon which the nation was founded. But the literacy test did not die so easily. The restrictionists once again raised cries for a literacy test after the assassination of President McKinley in 1901. The measure was passed by the House of Representatives but failed in the Senate.

As a result of the battle over the literacy test and the debate over immigration restriction that raged in the first decade of the 20th century, President Theodore Roosevelt established a congressional commission to review immigration policy in 1907 (much as he had done with the naturalization

In a cartoon that appeared in 1916 while Congress debated whether to adopt a literacy requirement for immigrants, Uncle Sam looks down on immigrants facing the literacy barrier. Representative John L. Burnett of Alabama, who had been a member of the U.S. Immigration Commission (1907–10), supported the exclusion of immigrants who could not pass a literacy test.

THE AMERICANESE WALL, AS CONGRESSMAN BURNETT WOULD BUILD IT.
UNCLE SAM: You're welcome in — if you can climb it!

Senator William P. Dillingham headed the congressionally appointed U.S. Immigration Commission, which issued a 42-volume report on the harmful effects of immigration in 1910. The Dillingham Report, as it became known, manipulated data to prove that immigration from southern and eastern Europe harmed the United States.

commission in 1905). Senator William P. Dillingham of Vermont headed the commission, which became known as the Dillingham Commission. The commission's 42-volume report, issued in 1911, asserted that the glut of unskilled immigrant laborers significantly harmed the economy and displaced American workers. The report, based on the racist assumption that the "new" immigrants from southern and central Europe were inferior to the "old" immigrants from northern and western Europe, also claimed that Italians and Jews were damaging the traditional Protestant, Anglo-Saxon stock that formed the foundation of the American populace. The Dillingham Commission concluded that the open-door policy of immigration weakened the nation and recommended that the literacy test should be employed to help keep out supposedly inferior aliens.

Nonetheless, the literacy test still was not adopted. Big businesses—such as New England textile mills and Chicago meat-packing plants—that employed many immigrants vigorously supported open immigration. The ever-increasing numbers of immigrant Americans were also vocal in denouncing restrictive measures. In 1912, Congress again passed an immigration bill establishing literacy as a requirement for admission into the country, and President William Howard Taft vetoed it, stating that the "sturdy but uneducated peasantry brought to this country and raised in an atmosphere of thrift and hard work" had contributed greatly to the growth of the nation.

Immigrants working in a Chicago meat-packing plant. Immigrant laborers filled many positions in factories, mines, and mills in the United States. Consequently, businesses lobbied for a liberal immigration policy.

The Era of Restriction

The issue of the literacy test came up again in 1915, and this time President Woodrow Wilson vetoed the bill. Like previous presidents who had struck down literacy legislation, Wilson found the bill hypocritical and unworthy of a powerful and benevolent nation founded on freedom. Wilson commented sharply that if the bill were enacted, "those who come seeking an opportunity [would] not be admitted unless they have already had one of the chief . . . opportunities they seek, the opportunity of education." However, when the measure came up yet again during World War I, Congress overrode Wilson's veto, and the Immigration Act of 1917 finally established a literacy requirement for entry into the United States. All new arrivals over 16 years of age who could not pass the literacy test were turned away. The act also added four new categories of inadmissible persons: alcoholics, stowaways, vagrants, and men entering for immoral purposes. In addition, the act nearly put an end to the entrance of Japanese people, reaffirming a 1907 gentlemen's agreement between the United States and Japan that had restricted Asian immigration.

World War I also prompted Americans to question the loyalty of the foreign-born inhabitants of the country, and such prominent Americans as former president Theodore Roosevelt attacked the "hyphenated Americans," such as Italian-American, Polish-American, and Russian-American immigrants. Since Germany was America's primary enemy during the war, German-American immigrants experienced intense discrimination during this period. Local authorities closed German-language schools, newspapers, and social organizations. The governor of Iowa even went as far as to declare that no language except English could be spoken in public places or over the telephone. Over the next several years, Congress passed several wartime immigration measures, such as the Anarchist Act of 1918, which provided for the deportation of foreign-born radicals, and the Deportation Act of 1919, which provided for the deportation of people convicted of spying for enemies of the United States.

In April 1918, a statue of Germania, which symbolizes Germany, is removed from a building in St. Paul, Minnesota. During both world wars, many people questioned the loyalty of German Americans, and some local authorities closed German-American schools, newspapers, and stores.

Although the restrictionists had finally won the battle over the controversial literacy test, they were still not satisfied. The temporary decrease in immigration caused by the war began to reverse itself in 1919 and 1920, and more than 800,000 immigrants—near the prewar average—arrived in 1921. Thousands of Europeans whose lives and jobs had been particularly affected by the devastation of the war came to the United States. The literacy test for which the restrictionists had fought so hard did not work as well as planned—the proportion of immigrants from southern and eastern Europe remained high. Immigrants to the United States generally were among the better educated in their place of origin. Italy even established schools in areas where many potential immigrants lived to help them pass the literacy test once they reached the United States.

In response to the failure of the literacy test to keep out the eastern and southern Europeans, a new group of extreme restrictionists who wanted to abolish immigration completely sprang up in the late 1910s. The 100 Per-centers (so called because they wanted to terminate all immigration) were fairly successful in spreading their message. The House of Representatives considered legislation banning all immigrants. But a more moderate measure was proposed in the Senate that would enable immigrants from the "desirable" parts of Europe—the northern and western countries such as England, Sweden, Denmark, and Norway—to immigrate while virtually stopping the flow of people from southern and eastern Europe.

Congress passed the moderate bill, and in 1921 President Warren Harding signed the Johnson Act—the first immigration law establishing a quota system based on national origin. The act set a limit of 355,000 European immigrants per year and limited the number of immigrants from each country to 3 percent of the number of foreign-born people of that nationality who were already residing in the United States at the time of the 1910 census. As a result, immigration from southern and eastern Europe was sharply curbed—to less than a quarter of the number who were admitted before the war.

Under the Johnson Act, spouses, parents, brothers, sisters, and children of U.S. citizens (or aliens who had applied for citizenship) received preferential treatment over other aliens seeking admission—within the limits of national quotas—in the interest of maintaining family unity. The act established nonquota categories, which included professional actors, artists, lecturers, singers, nurses, ministers, and professors. People in these groups could be admitted above and beyond the quotas for national groups to which they belonged but could not be admitted beyond the overall limit of 355,000.

THE ONLY WAY TO HANDLE IT.

Uncle Sam controls the gate that limits the influx of immigrants. Congress passed the Immigration Act of 1921 to prevent masses of Europeans from entering the country. The act set an annual limit of 355,000 European immigrants and restricted the number of immigrants from each country to 3 percent of the foreign-born people of that nationality living in the United States according to the 1910 census.

The Johnson Act was replaced in 1924 by an even more discriminatory and restrictive law. Congress passed the National Origins Act in order to maintain the "racial preponderance [of] the basic strain of our people." In other words, the government was trying to preserve America as a nation of Anglo-Saxon heritage. A limit of only 150,000 total immigrants (not including those from Canada and Mexico, who could still be admitted in unlimited numbers) could enter the country each year. The quota for each nationality was based on the proportion of people of that nationality residing in the United States at the time of the 1890 census in relation to the total population of the United States. Because relatively few southern and eastern Europeans had immigrated to the United States that early, the quotas for these countries were very small. Consequently, immigration from these parts of Europe practically ceased when the National Origins Act became effective in 1929. For example, the quota for Italy, which had sent more than 200,000 people in 1920 (the year before quotas were instituted), was cut to a maximum of 42,000 under the 1921 act and fewer than 4,000 under the 1924 act. The National Origins Act required all

Republican representative Albert Johnson, sponsor of immigration legislation in 1921 and 1924, was one of the leaders of the crusade for restrictive immigration laws.

immigrants to obtain a visa from an American consulate in their home country, which allowed government officials to deny admission to even more prospective immigrants.

The National Origins Act put an end to one of the original principles on which the nation was founded—that the United States should be a place of opportunity for the oppressed peoples of the world. Senator Albert Johnson of Washington, chairman of the House Committee on Immigration, summarized the intent of the restrictive policies of the 1924 act:

> The United States is our land. If it was not the land of our fathers,
> at least it may be, and it should be, the land of our children. We
> intend to maintain it so. The day of unalloyed welcome to all peoples,
> the day of indiscriminate acceptance of all races, has definitely
> ended.

During the depression, immigration quotas often went unfilled because the lack of economic opportunities in the United States discouraged many prospective immigrants and because immigrants already in the country began returning to their homeland to pursue better prospects. Also, in 1930, the unemployment crisis prompted President Herbert Hoover to order the State Department to deny visas by frequently applying the immigration clause excluding those likely to become public charges. Consequently, by 1932 the number of people leaving the United States exceeded the number of immigrants: 35,576 people entered that year, but more than 100,000 returned to their homelands. Only 500,000 foreign-born people entered America during the 1930s, the lowest total for a decade since the 1820s.

In 1933, President Franklin Roosevelt changed the structure of the bureaucracy by issuing Executive Order 6166. It consolidated the Bureau of Immigration and Naturalization into the Immigration and Naturalization Service, headed by a commissioner who reported to the secretary of labor. Congress had transferred the Bureau of Immigration and Naturalization in 1913 from the Department of Labor and Commerce to the new Department of Labor (formed when the original department was split into two separate agencies—the other being the Department of Commerce).

FDR's secretary of labor, Frances Perkins, found the INS in disarray when she took office in 1933. During her first day on the job, Perkins—the first female cabinet member—quickly discovered widespread disorganization, mismanagement, and outright corruption. Although many of the officials she met claimed to be in charge of immigration, nobody seemed to know what anyone else was doing. Despite the declining number of immigrants, the bureau had more than 3,600 employees and a budget of almost $10 million. But even more alarming was Perkins's discovery of the so-called Section 24 squad. The squad, named after the section of the 1917 Immigration Act that established it, was charged with enforcing the law prohibiting contract labor. But because the practice of contract labor was rare during the depression, the group was given a new assignment—the location and deportation of illegal aliens. The leaders of Section 24 interpreted this directive as a license to harass and detain suspected aliens without necessarily following the strictures of due process of law as guaranteed by the Fifth and Fourteenth amendments to the Constitution. For example, in 1932 a group of agents forcibly entered several apartment buildings in Detroit without warrants and arrested more than 600 people. Only two of the people detained were found to be subject to deportation. The Section 24 agents were civil servants and could not be fired without charges being brought against each one for misconduct in performing his or her work. However, Perkins was able to eliminate Section 24 by intentionally failing to submit to Congress the annual request for funding of the squad, a request that would certainly have been granted. Section 24 was thus abolished for lack of funds.

Frances Perkins, the first female cabinet member, served as secretary of labor from 1933 to 1945. In overseeing the INS, she disposed of its notorious Section 24 squad, a group of INS agents who had been unlawfully harassing and detaining suspected illegal aliens.

In 1940, Roosevelt, during a broad reorganization of the executive branch, transferred the INS from the Department of Labor to the Justice Department, placing it under the supervision of the attorney general, where it remains today. Roosevelt chose to move the INS to the Department of Justice because the war in Europe had engendered concern over the possibility of an influx of foreign spies and subversives. The enforcement of laws requiring alien registration and fingerprinting became the focus of the INS. These activities were more closely related to the duties of the enforcement agencies, such as the Federal Bureau of Investigation (FBI), in the Justice Department.

During most of Roosevelt's administration (1933–45), immigration policies were rigorously enforced and became more restrictive. In 1938, Congress defeated a bill that would have admitted as refugees 20,000 Jewish children suffering under Nazi persecution. Sponsor families in the United States were willing to take in all of the children, but the measure died because 20,000 immigrants exceeded the total quota allotted for Germany under the 1924 act. The small number of children who were allowed to come still had to pass the other entry requirements, such as medical fitness, and many failed and were turned away. In 1940, in response to the war in Europe, President Roosevelt signed the Alien Registration Act, which required that all aliens living in the United States be registered with the INS and fingerprinted. The act also extended the grounds for deportation of suspected subversives.

Perhaps the greatest tragedy of the war years was the detention of 112,000 West Coast Japanese Americans from 1942 until 1945. The unfounded fear of Japanese Americans that resulted from the Japanese attack on the U.S. naval base in Pearl Harbor, Hawaii, led to the roundup and internment of completely innocent citizens in camps. More than 40 years later, in 1988, President Ronald Reagan signed into law a bill officially apologizing for the internment of Japanese Americans and promising to pay each of the 60,000 surviving victims $20,000 as compensation for lost freedom, jobs, and belongings. As of late 1989, however, none of the detainees had been paid because no money had been appropriated in the federal budget.

World War II also brought about some loosening of immigration restrictions. Because labor was desperately needed while Americans were fighting overseas, the demand for alien workers increased. The United States negotiated the *bracero* (from the Spanish word meaning day laborer) program with

In April 1942, the last residents of Japanese ancestry in Redondo Beach, California, gather a few of their possessions before being moved to an internment camp for the duration of World War II. By November 1942, approximately 112,000 Japanese Americans were detained in camps located in isolated regions of California, Arizona, Utah, Idaho, Colorado, Wyoming, and Arkansas.

Mexico, British Honduras, Barbados, and Jamaica, which allowed thousands of foreign laborers to reside temporarily in the United States, primarily to work on the country's farms. (The bracero program survived until 1964, establishing a pattern of migration that continues today despite the change in U.S. policy.) Because China had become an ally of the United States against Japan, Congress, in 1943, repealed the Chinese Exclusion Act, thereby allowing foreign-born Chinese to become American citizens for the first time since 1882.

When World War II ended in 1945, many American servicemen and women returned home with families from overseas. The 1946 War Brides Act permitted 120,000 alien husbands, wives, and children to enter the United States. The Displaced Persons Act (1948) provided for the entrance of 400,000 refugees displaced by the war. However, these two acts were special

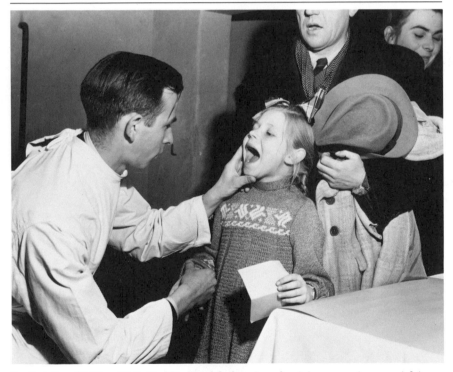

In October 1948, a U.S. Public Health Service physician examines a girl in Bremerhaven, Germany. She was among the first group of displaced people who departed for the United States under the Displaced Persons Act of 1948, which allowed 400,000 refugees to immigrate to the United States.

Famed film comedian and director Charlie Chaplin arrives in London with his wife Oona in 1953 after voluntarily surrendering his U.S. alien registration card, giving up his status as a permanent resident. If Chaplin had returned to the United States during the McCarthy era (1950–54), he would have faced a congressional investigation into allegations that he was a Communist sympathizer.

measures enacted as a result of the emergencies of wartime and did not affect the existing national-origins quota system.

American politics became very conservative in the years immediately following World War II. Senator Joseph McCarthy's "witch-hunts" for Communist sympathizers created an uproar, and a growing fear of the Soviet Union consumed many Americans. Inevitably, this climate influenced immigration policy. The Internal Security Act of 1950 greatly increased the power of the government to exclude and deport aliens who were deemed potentially dangerous to U.S. national security.

In 1952, Congress, led by Senator Pat McCarran of Nevada and Representative Francis Walter of Pennsylvania, passed a new immigration bill. Officially titled the Immigration and Nationality Act, but better known as the McCarran-Walter Act, this law consolidated all the existing immigration statutes into one piece of legislation, and it remains the basic law governing immigration. It established a limit of 160,000 entrants per year from countries in the Eastern Hemisphere. (There was still no limit for the Western Hemisphere.) The countries of northern and Western Europe received more than 85 percent of the total annual quota. The act established, for the first time, a system of preference categories that would determine which immigrants would be allowed to enter. This meant that immediate relatives of American citizens and people who had special talents or skills that would benefit the country would be given special consideration among the other applicants for immigration. It also repealed the Japanese exclusion policies that had been in effect since 1907, allowing small numbers of Asians to apply for immigration. But in spite of these changes, the McCarran-Walter Act retained the discriminatory national-origins quota system of the 1924 law.

President Harry Truman opposed the act, and Congress had to pass it over his veto. In rejecting the bill, Truman vehemently stated, "The basis of this quota system was false and unworthy in 1924. It is even worse now. . . . It is incredible to me that, in this year of 1952, we should again be enacting into law such a slur on the patriotism, the capacity, and the decency of a large part of our citizenry." The McCarran-Walter Act proved broadly unpopular because it retained the national-origins quota system. The American Bar Association, the American Federation of Labor and Congress of Industrial Organizations (AFL-CIO), and even the Daughters of the American Revolution called for changes in the law.

The Era of Liberalization

In 1963, President John F. Kennedy submitted to Congress an immigration reform bill, calling for the repeal of the national-origins quota system because it was "without basis in either logic or reason . . . it discriminates among applicants for admission into the United States on the basis of accident of birth." It was appropriate that Kennedy would press for reform in immigration policy. Five years earlier, he had written *A Nation of Immigrants*, a book that criticized the national-origins quota system. His grandparents were Irish immigrants, and he was the first Roman Catholic president. His family's success symbolized America's reputation as a land of opportunity, and his election in 1960 signaled that attitudes were changing in the United States. The early 1960s was also a period of increasing prosperity and an era in which civil rights legislation—declaring race as an illegal factor to consider in providing employment, housing, and public accommodations—was enacted. Also, the United States wanted to develop good relations with the newly independent nations of Africa and Asia.

Kennedy was assassinated in 1963, before he could see an immigration bill enacted into law. But President Lyndon B. Johnson embraced Kennedy's immigration policies, and in 1965 he signed legislation that amended the McCarran-Walter Act. The Hart-Celler Act, which took effect in 1969, abolished the national-origins quotas and set a total immigration limit of 170,000 people for all countries outside the Western Hemisphere, with no more than 20,000 from any single country. The 1965 act also established, for the first time, a limit of 120,000 total immigrants from the Western Hemisphere, with no individual country limit. Consequently, the Hart-Celler Act increased immigration from countries whose quotas had previously been small—for example, China, India, Greece, and Portugal. The amendments continued the system of preferences for skilled workers and immediate relatives of American citizens. While signing the Hart-Celler Act, Johnson summed up the discriminatory immigration policies that had actively kept out certain nationalities and ethnic groups in the previous 50 years, saying "the system violated the basic

President John F. Kennedy (center) and Vice President Lyndon B. Johnson outside the White House. After becoming president upon Kennedy's assassination in November 1963, Johnson sponsored Kennedy's immigration reform amendments, which Congress passed in 1965. The amendments replaced the discriminatory national-origins quota system and allowed as many as 20,000 immigrants from each country, with an annual overall limit of 170,000.

principle of American democracy—the principle that values and rewards each man on the basis of his merit. . . . [I]t has been un-American."

Although the 1965 amendments represented a great step forward for fair immigration policies, they created a whole new set of problems. During the 1970s and 1980s, refugees and illegal aliens presented the greatest problems in immigration policy. In the early 1960s approximately 60,000 aliens entered the United States illegally each year; by the end of the 1970s, more than 1 million entered annually. The limit on immigration from Latin America, particularly Mexico, meant that many prospective immigrants and itinerant workers who wanted to come to the United States (and who had been free to do so under previous laws) were now forced to wait years before their application to immigrate was approved. In 1976, Congress passed another amendment that made it even more difficult for Mexicans to immigrate. The amendment established the same 20,000-immigrant-per-year limit for countries in the Western Hemisphere—including Mexico—that applied to Eastern Hemisphere countries. In 1978, the total hemispheric limits were abolished, and a worldwide limit of 290,000 immigrants per year (with no more than 20,000 per country) was established; it remains in force.

In 1980, Congress passed the Refugee Act, eliminating previous restrictions that granted entry primarily to refugees from Communist countries or the Middle East. Under the act, a *refugee* is a person who has been persecuted, or has a well-founded fear of persecution, on account of his or her race, religion, nationality, membership in a particular social group, or political opinion. Aliens temporarily on American soil who fear that returning to their homeland would endanger their life may request asylum, which would allow them to remain in the United States permanently. Each request for asylum (sometimes known as defecting) is decided on a case-by-case basis to determine whether the applicant has the requisite well-founded fear of persecution.

The 1980 act standardized the procedures for granting permanent residence to all refugees and aliens seeking asylum; they are now admitted without regard to national origin. The act permits the entry of 50,000 refugees each year but allows the president, in consultation with Congress, to increase the annual quota. In 1980 and 1981, the first 2 years after the law was enacted, President Reagan authorized the entry of 231,400 refugees each year. In 1989, the annual allotment was set at 116,500, and President Bush proposed setting the number at 125,000 for 1990.

Because many people do not want to wait the years it takes to immigrate legally, some try to cross the United States's borders illegally, and others—such as tourists and students—remain in the country beyond the expiration date of their temporary visas. Illegal entry has become the major problem facing the INS today. In 1976, the INS apprehended more than a million illegal aliens—a record number in a single year—but the INS has difficulty preventing these crossings because illegal immigrants vastly outnumber INS inspectors and Border Patrol officers. For many poor Mexicans, job opportunities are far greater in America than in their own country, and many are willing to risk capture by the INS (and even death during a dangerous crossing). The INS cannot determine how many illegals actually make it to the United States, but the number of apprehensions hovers around the 1 million mark every year. In 1986, the INS made more than 1.7 million apprehensions, the all-time record.

Congress passed the Immigration Reform and Control Act (IRCA) in 1986 in an attempt to slow down the flow of illegal immigration. The act provides stiff penalties, such as large fines and prison terms, for employers who hire undocumented aliens. Employers must ask new employees to provide documentation that they are U.S. citizens or aliens eligible to work in the United

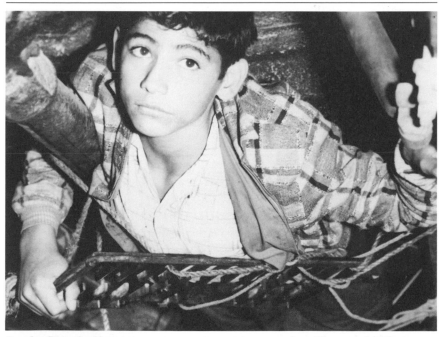

Border Patrol officers uncover an attempt to smuggle a 13-year-old Mexican boy into the United States under a car. In 1978, the INS established a separate division that investigates cases involving the smuggling of aliens into the United States.

A Century of Immigration

Tens of millions of Europeans, Asians, Latinos and others joined the U.S. "melting pot" in

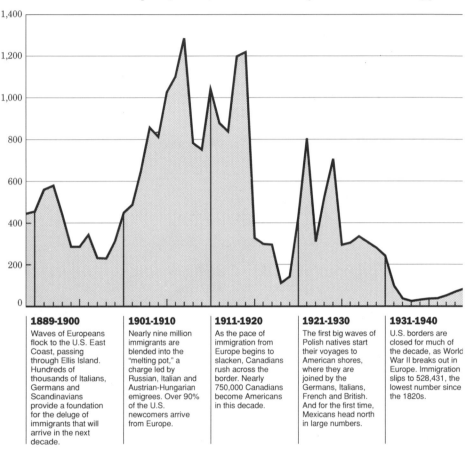

1889-1900	1901-1910	1911-1920	1921-1930	1931-1940
Waves of Europeans flock to the U.S. East Coast, passing through Ellis Island. Hundreds of thousands of Italians, Germans and Scandinavians provide a foundation for the deluge of immigrants that will arrive in the next decade.	Nearly nine million immigrants are blended into the "melting pot," a charge led by Russian, Italian and Austrian-Hungarian emigrees. Over 90% of the U.S. newcomers arrive from Europe.	As the pace of immigration from Europe begins to slacken, Canadians rush across the border. Nearly 750,000 Canadians become Americans in this decade.	The first big waves of Polish natives start their voyages to American shores, where they are joined by the Germans, Italians, French and British. And for the first time, Mexicans head north in large numbers.	U.S. borders are closed for much of the decade, as World War II breaks out in Europe. Immigration slips to 528,431, the lowest number since the 1820s.

States. IRCA quickly produced tangible results. Because employers are now more reluctant to hire illegal aliens, there is less incentive for them to cross into the United States. Apprehensions of illegals fell to 1.2 million in 1987 and to 940,000 in 1988. While some of the drop in the number of apprehensions may be attributed to IRCA's amnesty program—many illegal aliens changed their status to temporary residents by applying for amnesty and were no longer subject to apprehension—the threat of employer sanctions has reduced the availability of jobs for illegal aliens.

the past hundred years. (Number of immigrants in thousands)

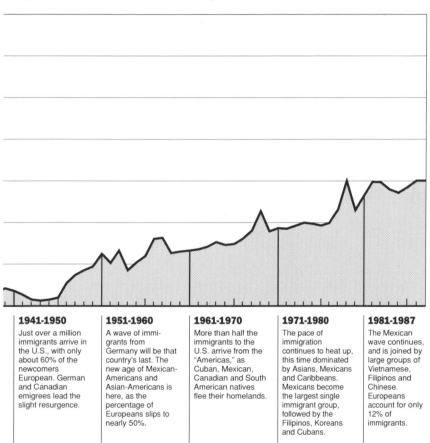

1941-1950	1951-1960	1961-1970	1971-1980	1981-1987
Just over a million immigrants arrive in the U.S., with only about 60% of the newcomers European. German and Canadian emigrees lead the slight resurgence.	A wave of immigrants from Germany will be that country's last. The new age of Mexican-Americans and Asian-Americans is here, as the percentage of Europeans slips to nearly 50%.	More than half the immigrants to the U.S. arrive from the "Americas," as Cuban, Mexican, Canadian and South American natives flee their homelands.	The pace of immigration continues to heat up, this time dominated by Asians, Mexicans and Caribbeans. Mexicans become the largest single immigrant group, followed by the Filipinos, Koreans and Cubans.	The Mexican wave continues, and is joined by large groups of Vietnamese, Filipinos and Chinese. Europeans account for only 12% of immigrants.

As the responsibilities of the INS grow to meet the increasingly complex needs of immigration policy, the functions and agenda of the agency will continue to change. From the policy of open-door immigration envisioned by George Washington and Thomas Jefferson through the years of restrictive quotas at the turn of the 20th century to the current system that admits peoples of all nations, the history of U.S. immigration policy reflects the developing attitudes and circumstances of this country and the rest of the world.

A Border Patrol officer, riding an all-terrain vehicle (ATV), keeps watch at the Mexican border. The Border Patrol, a division of the INS, tries to ensure that no one enters the United States without following the proper procedures, and it apprehends aliens who have slipped into the country illegally.

FOUR

Inside the INS

The INS has been a division of the U.S. Department of Justice since 1940 and, therefore, falls under the direction of the attorney general. The attorney general—the nation's chief legal officer—represents the United States in litigation, appears before the Supreme Court in particularly important cases, and advises the president and the heads of department in the executive branch on legal matters.

The INS administers and enforces laws relating to the admission, exclusion, deportation, and naturalization of aliens. It works to prevent undocumented entry into the United States; investigates, apprehends, and removes undocumented aliens; and supervises the operations of the U.S. Border Patrol.

The Commissioner's Office

The attorney general has delegated the administration of the diverse programs of the INS to a commissioner, who is selected by the president and approved by the Senate. The commissioner appoints a deputy commissioner, who assists the commissioner in all his or her duties. The deputy commissioner oversees the operations of the INS program officers and field officers and assumes the duties of the commissioner when he or she is unable to fulfill them.

Three departments report directly to the commissioner and the deputy commissioner: the Office of the General Counsel, the Office of the Chief of Staff, and the Office of Congressional and Public Affairs.

Richard Thornburgh was appointed attorney general in 1988. The attorney general, who is responsible for the administration and enforcement of immigration laws, has delegated to the commissioner of the INS the authority to carry out the country's immigration policy.

The Office of the General Counsel

The Office of the General Counsel, the legal branch of the INS, employs approximately 40 of the INS's 400 attorneys, who represent the INS in court and advise INS officials on the legal consequences of their operations. Whenever someone brings suit against the INS, attorneys from the General Counsel's office defend the agency. They also prosecute cases involving immigration fraud. In such cases, attorneys in the Office of the General Counsel work closely with INS investigators, who are responsible for gathering evidence and related information. The Office of the General Counsel also keeps abreast of changes in legislation affecting immigration policy. To inform the rest of the agency of changes in the law, the office publishes the *General Counsel's Law Bulletin* every month.

In 1986, the Office of the General Counsel began to participate in a program that enabled lawyers from the INS to work in the Office of U.S. Attorneys (a Justice Department division that handles federal criminal matters) in regions experiencing a high concentration of immigration crime. The Special Assistant United States Attorneys Program resulted in more efficient and effective enforcement of crimes involving aliens, such as drug smuggling, because INS lawyers used their expertise in immigration law to help the U.S. Attorneys.

The Office of the Chief of Staff

The Office of the Chief of Staff assists the commissioner with the internal administrative work of the INS. The Chief of Staff also coordinates the operations of the Office of Plans and Analysis and Office of Foreign Operations.

The Office of Plans and Analysis advises the commissioner on the development and adoption of INS policies, plans, and programs. It conducts research on immigration issues such as the apprehension of people smuggling aliens into the country and the setting of bond for aliens awaiting deportation hearings. The Plans and Analysis staff also advises division heads on immigration topics to assist them in enforcing immigration laws. For example, they helped develop techniques to assist INS officers in the Examinations division in detecting marriage fraud.

The Chief of Staff also supervises the Foreign Operations division, which contains the Office of Refugees, Asylum, and Parole and the Overseas Offices. The Office of Refugees, Asylum, and Parole grants admission to refugees from foreign countries and asylum to aliens already in America. Citizens living in another country who are displaced by war or other circumstances that endanger their existence may petition to relocate to America as refugees.

71

Because decisions regarding such people are often decisions of life and death, the INS must handle these matters very carefully. In dealing with refugee cases, the INS works closely with the State Department, which ultimately decides who will be granted refugee status.

The INS has also established a network of offices around the world to provide more efficient service. There are three overseas district offices—in Rome, Mexico City, and Bangkok—and numerous suboffices in cities throughout the world. The foreign field offices, like their counterparts in the United States, are responsible for implementing all INS programs on a local level. The overseas offices work closely with the American embassies in their respective cities. Activities of the Foreign Operations division include interviewing and investigating prospective refugees and processing their applications. INS overseas offices also grant visas under special circumstances. The State Department normally grants visas but will delegate its authority to INS

Fourteen-year-old Gata Kamsky (left) and his father, Rustram, appear at a news conference at New York's Marshall Chess Club in April 1989 to explain why they decided to seek political asylum in the United States. The younger Kamsky, the Soviet Union's leading young chess player, chose to defect so he could play in more chess tournaments.

overseas offices to ease the burden caused by the numerous requests for visas in some countries.

In 1986, the INS launched a preinspection program in Shannon, Ireland. The preinspection program was designed to screen Irish travelers *before* they reached the United States, thereby reducing the congestion at already busy inspection points in America. In this program, visa applications, medical records, and accompanying documents are checked for authenticity and accuracy. Any prospective immigrants whose credentials are suspect are turned back before they ever board aircraft headed for America. The success of this program is encouraging to the INS for two reasons. First, the effective screening of applicants saves the government the time and expense of arresting, detaining, and deporting aliens found to be in the United States illegally. Second, successful screening at a given overseas port of departure serves as a deterrent to others who would illegally emigrate to America through that same port. In addition, the INS hopes that preinspection programs will foster better relations between the United States and foreign countries.

The Office of Congressional and Public Affairs

The Office of Congressional and Public Affairs serves as the link between the INS and Congress. It also works with other government agencies, state and local governments, the media, and the public. This office deals directly with members of Congress to coordinate support for proposed legislation that the INS supports. In a typical year, the office fields more than 30,000 inquiries from Congress and prepares approximately 5,000 written replies to congressional requests for information concerning the status of particular cases and requirements of immigration law and procedures. Congressional and Public Affairs also produces such publications as the commission's newsletter to all INS employees and the annual report of the INS.

Programs

The INS is organized into four program areas: Examinations, Enforcement, Management, and Information Systems. An associate commissioner, who reports directly to the commissioner's office, heads each program.

Examinations

The mission of the Examinations program is to ensure that immigration laws are administered properly and effectively. It inspects all aliens entering the

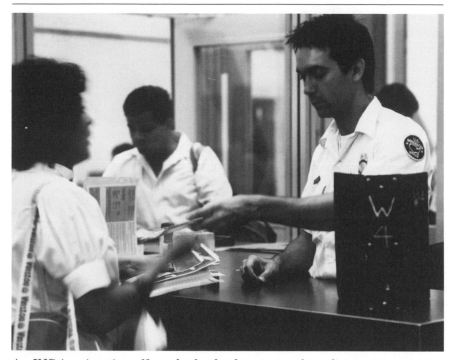

An INS immigration officer checks the documents of an alien arriving at John F. Kennedy International Airport in New York City. The INS inspects all entering aliens over 14 years old to determine whether they are admissible under immigration law. After World War II, the spread of relatively cheap air transportation ended mass immigration via ship. By 1960, the majority of INS inspections activity occurred at airports and along land borders.

United States and processes applications for naturalization after immigrants have become permanent residents. The divisions of Adjudications and Naturalization, Inspections, and Legalization are part of the Examinations program.

The Adjudications and Naturalization division processes and judges all applications for naturalization. Examiners analyze applications to determine whether they are valid or fraudulent. Judging the validity of marriages between American citizens and aliens, who would then automatically become eligible for permanent residence, presents examiners with a particularly delicate matter. If, in the judgment of an examiner, the sole purpose of a marriage is to enable an alien to become a U.S. resident, the spouse can either be prohibited from entering the United States (if he or she is outside the country) or can be deported.

In 1986, the division conducted a survey that found approximately 30 percent of all such marriages to be fraudulent. The Marriage Fraud Amendments Act of 1986, which the division proposed to Congress through the Office of Congressional and Public Affairs, seeks to discourage fraudulent marriages. The act grants a couple permission to live in the United States for two years (conditional residence), and then the INS reviews the case. If the alien cannot prove that the marriage has been in good faith, he or she can be deported.

The Executive Office for Immigration Review, a separate division of the Justice Department, employs immigration judges who rule on cases involving the exclusion or deportation of an alien. Their decisions may be appealed to the Board of Immigration Appeals, which analyzes and interprets immigration laws and regulations to ensure that they are applied uniformly throughout the United States. The Board of Immigration Appeals is the final INS arbiter of an immigrant's status. Decisions of the board may be appealed to a federal district court.

An immigration judge conducts a hearing to determine the immigration status of an alien. Immigration judges rule on cases involving the exclusion or deportation of aliens. Aliens can appeal INS decisions in federal district courts.

Border Patrol officers inspect a truck entering the United States. In addition to apprehending aliens crossing the border illegally, Border Patrol officers are involved in stopping the flow of illegal drugs into the country.

The Inspections division, which is part of the Examinations program, is one of the most visible arms of the INS. Inspections is responsible for checking the millions of people arriving at airports, seaports, and other points of entry to ensure that they are entering the country legally. In 1988, nearly 200 million aliens entered the United States. INS inspectors determine whether arrivals are foreigners on a temporary visit or immigrants seeking permanent residence. People who lack proper credentials for entry—for example, a visa and passport, immigration or refugee documents, or a labor certificate—are held for further questioning and may be detained.

In order to curb the number of immigrants illegally entering through U.S. ports of entry, the INS often teams up with other government agencies. At inspection points, for example, the INS inspectors work side by side with agents of the United States Customs Service (a division of the Treasury Department) and sometimes with agents of two agencies within the Justice Department—the FBI and the Drug Enforcement Administration (DEA). Interagency cooperation is necessary at entry points because inspection officials may face incidents ranging from drug smuggling to terrorist actions and hostage taking.

The Legalization division administers the legalization and special agricultural worker programs established by IRCA, which provided certain illegal aliens with the opportunity to become U.S. residents. The division processed the 3 million applications for legal status filed during the application periods. It now supervises and provides necessary information to aliens who were granted temporary resident status. It also processes applications for permanent residence under the second phase of the program.

Enforcement

Whereas the Examinations program is concerned with inspecting and processing legal immigrants, the job of the Enforcement program is to identify and process people trying to enter the country illegally. Officers of the Enforcement program also investigate crimes that involve illegal immigrants or immigration fraud. For example, the Investigations division gathers information used to prosecute employers who violate immigration law by hiring undocumented aliens.

In 1985, Investigations division officers closed their case against Bhagwan Shree Rajneesh, an Indian guru (religious leader) who had settled in a small Oregon community with his followers. Complaints alleging illegal conduct led investigators to scrutinize the activities of Rajneesh. They discovered that he and his group planned to bring an additional 400 of their followers into the

Bhagwan Shree Rajneesh, a guru from India, agreed to leave the United States after pleading guilty to two counts of immigration fraud in November 1985. INS investigators uncovered evidence of Rajneesh's scheme to arrange fraudulent marriages that would have allowed more of his followers to enter the country.

United States illegally by arranging fraudulent marriages between them and American citizens. INS agents and other federal and state law-enforcement officials exposed the scheme, and in return for pleading guilty to engineering the scam, Rajneesh and his followers were allowed to leave the country. Though Rajneesh was the butt of many jokes about his flamboyant life-style (he owned dozens of Rolls-Royces), his activities constituted a serious violation of immigration law.

The Border Patrol is the best-known division in the Enforcement program. Officially established as part of the INS in 1924 (when the INS was still part of the Department of Labor), the Border Patrol was created in response to the large-scale smuggling of illegal aliens by boat to states on the Gulf of Mexico. In 1925, the patrol was expanded to cover land borders as well. Today, the mission of the Border Patrol remains the same—to ensure that no one enters the United States without following the proper procedures and to apprehend those who have managed to enter America illegally. With approximately 3,500 agents and thousands of miles of borders to cover, the patrol has an immensely difficult task. During the 1986 fiscal year (October 1985 through September 1986), the patrol caught more than 1.7 million illegal aliens, the vast majority of whom were Mexican. (Approximately 95 percent of the patrol's activity takes place on the U.S.-Mexican border.) During the same period, Border Patrol officers also made 1,300 narcotics seizures, preventing more than 133,000 pounds of marijuana and 2,500 pounds of cocaine from entering the United States.

The high stakes involved in illegal immigration have driven criminals to devise highly organized networks to smuggle people across the border. In response, in 1978 the INS established a division within the Enforcement program that specifically investigates cases involving the smuggling of aliens into the country. Yet, because of its profitability, the incidence of alien smuggling increased during the 1980s. According to the INS, the charge in 1989 for smuggling an alien into the United States from the Eastern Hemisphere was about $25,000; from South America, about $10,000; from Central America, $2,000; and from Mexico, a relatively inexpensive $800. The INS antismuggling staff works closely with other government agencies, such as the FBI and the DEA.

Agents in the Anti-smuggling division scored a major victory in May 1989 when they arrested six people suspected of being ringleaders of an operation that smuggled hundreds of illegal aliens into the country. The aliens—mostly Chinese—were frequently stuffed three or four at a time into trunks of cars and driven across the Canadian border into New York. Once in America, they were either put to work (quite possibly for their entire life) repaying the people who fronted the smugglers' costs or were coerced into joining one of the Asian gangs that dominate the illegal heroin market in New York City. The suspects, if convicted, could be sentenced to 5 years in prison and fined up to $250,000 each.

The Detention and Deportation division is the branch of the Enforcement program that detains aliens if their immigration status is uncertain and expels aliens who are in the United States illegally. When the Border Patrol apprehends an illegal alien or when the INS determines that an alien should be deported, his or her case then becomes the responsibility of the Detention and Deportation division. Deportation hearings are held before an immigration judge who can order the deportation, suspend it, or allow the alien to leave voluntarily. Aliens who are deported are transported at government expense back to their countries of origin or to a third country that agrees to accept them.

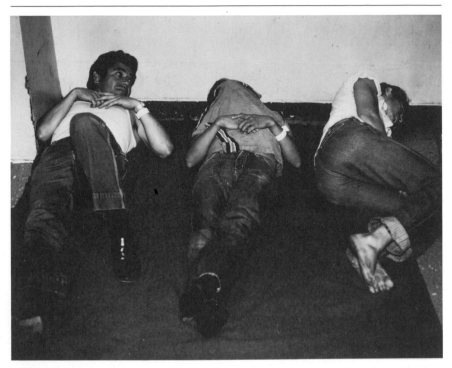

Illegal aliens await deportation. The Detention and Deportation division of the INS holds aliens whose immigration status is uncertain and expels aliens who are in the country illegally.

Detention and Deportation also oversees seven INS detention centers—including the Oakdale Federal Alien Detention Center in Louisiana, which the INS operates jointly with the Bureau of Prisons. It also uses state, county, and local jails to detain aliens awaiting deportation or exclusion hearings.

Information Systems

The Information Systems program develops and manages the information resources that are needed by the other program areas. This program, supervised by the associate commissioner for Information Systems, is divided into three divisions: data systems (which handles the flow of information between INS offices), records systems (which maintains the files on immigrants, refugees, and other aliens), and systems integration (which installs and designs the computer systems). The divisions are responsible for finding ways to make information processing and retrieval more efficient.

The data systems division developed a useful innovation in 1983. The National Automated Immigration Lookout System (NAILS) makes vital information available to immigration agents who inspect aliens arriving in the United States. Names and other information—such as physical appearance and aliases—about known undesirable aliens are immediately available by computer to INS officers at major ports of entry such as New York, Miami, Buffalo, Chicago, and San Francisco.

The computer room at INS headquarters in Washington, D.C. The INS uses computers to keep case files on immigrants and other aliens in the country. It also maintains a computerized list, the National Automated Immigration Lookout System (NAILS), that contains approximately 40,000 names of people barred from the United States. Criminals, suspected terrorists, and other undesirable aliens appear in the INS "lookout book."

Management

The Management program, headed by an associate commissioner, is the administrative branch of the INS. It creates budgets, works to improve efficiency, and handles the agency's personnel matters. Like most other government agencies, the INS must find ways to operate with a limited budget. The Management program has adopted automated systems to increase efficiency. Many procedures that had been performed manually are now being done more quickly and cheaply by machine. For example, an inventory-control system for automated weapons, initiated in 1986, helps keep track of the firearms used by different INS divisions. The Office of the Comptroller is responsible for budgeting and accounting. In its search for ways to stretch the budgeted dollars, the Office of the Comptroller's recent initiatives have included revising fee schedules for immigration application forms so that they more accurately cover the costs of services and working with the Treasury Department to ensure a more efficient transfer of funds between different departments within the INS.

Field Offices

To perform its many functions, the INS has established a system of field offices throughout the country. The United States is divided into four regions, each having a regional office administered by a regional commissioner, who reports directly to the commissioner's office in Washington. The four regions (and the location of their respective offices) are Northern (St. Paul, Minnesota), Southern (Dallas, Texas), Eastern (Burlington, Vermont), and Western (San Pedro, California). Each of the 4 regions is divided into domestic districts, and each of the 33 districts has a district director who is responsible to his or her regional commissioner. Each domestic district, in turn, is split up into suboffices that carry out the objectives of all INS programs.

The field officers in the domestic districts and suboffices enforce immigration laws on the street level. For example, upon arrival at a U.S. port, all aliens over the age of 14 are inspected by an agent of the Inspections suboffice, who determines whether they are admissible. If the inspector decides that the alien is admissible, then the person can enter the country. If the inspector finds that the alien should not be admitted, the person must return home or request a hearing before an immigration judge to explain why he or she should be admitted. There are 33 categories of exclusion that prevent certain aliens from entering the country—for example, aliens who are insane, who are stowaways,

Evidence of forged signatures. Because of the limited number of immigration visas available each year, some aliens attempt to use forged documents to enter or stay in the United States. In 1989, the INS began printing alien registration cards with a special ink to foil forgers who produce counterfeit cards that sell for as much as $10,000 on the black market.

or who have been excluded or deported within the preceding year. If the immigration judge confirms the inspection officer's decision, the alien is required to leave the country. While awaiting the hearing, aliens are usually not detained unless they present forged documents or none at all. Officers of the Detention and Deportation suboffice handle the detention and deportation of aliens.

The Border Patrol consists of 20 field offices, called sectors, each headed by a chief patrol agent. The sectors serve as the bases from which the patrol carries out its mission of apprehending illegal aliens and preventing the smuggling of illicit drugs.

A Border Patrol officer uses a night-vision telescope to detect illegal crossings at the U.S.-Mexican border. The INS employs the latest technology to apprehend aliens entering the United States illegally.

FIVE

The INS Today

The INS now faces problems that could hardly have been imagined when the agency was created. The volume and scope of its responsibilities strains the $1 billion annual budget and the more than 14,000 employees of the INS. Millions of foreigners apply to immigrate to the United States. Illegal aliens, refugees, and those seeking asylum flood the country. INS officers at the national borders are engaged in the increasingly violent war against drug smuggling.

Illegal immigration presents a nearly unmanageable crisis. The Border Patrol, the first line of defense in the battle against illegal immigrants, now employs a wide range of technologies to prevent aliens from sneaking across America's 8,000 miles of international boundaries. In order to track aliens who travel at night, the patrol now uses infrared imaging devices. Unlike the human eye, infrared scopes detect heat rather than light. Although people usually cannot be seen in the dark, they always radiate heat. By detecting body heat, the scopes allow officers to see at night. The patrol has recently deployed an image-enhancement vehicle, a truck equipped with infrared monitors and cameras mounted on a 30-foot-long retractable mast that feed infrared images to the monitors. The system enables Border Patrol officers to use infrared technology over a greater geographical area. The INS hopes to have 10 of these vehicles in operation in 1990. The Border Patrol also uses advanced seismic sensors, which detect vibrations in the ground, to track movement

A Border Patrol officer saddles his horse before going out on patrol. The Border Patrol uses horses and all-terrain vehicles to track illegal aliens over rough landscape near the borders.

across the border. Low-light-level television cameras have been installed at various strategic points along the border to help officers keep watch for alien traffic.

Because patrol personnel must cover a great amount of area quickly, they use a variety of vehicles: specially modified automobiles for high-speed pursuit, four-wheel-drive trucks and three- and four-wheel all-terrain vehicles (ATVs) on rugged desert landscapes, and small airplanes and helicopters for aerial surveillance. Despite the modernization of Border Patrol equipment and techniques, patrol officers still employ methods that cavalry scouts and cowboys used in the 1800s. Because there are many treacherous spots where even small and agile ATVs cannot reach, patrol officers often ride on horseback, especially when tracking debris and individual footprints left behind by aliens. Such tracking is referred to as sign cutting and is a highly developed skill originally mastered by Native Americans. Sometimes officers follow the tracks for several days before they catch aliens and turn them over to the Detention and Deportation division. Old and new, the methods have started to pay off. In 1986, the INS apprehended a record 1,767,400 illegal aliens, most of whom were caught by the Border Patrol.

Organized crime, which is becoming increasingly involved with the illegal drug trade, presents the INS with another difficult problem. Although the United States has an official agency—the DEA—designated to deal with drug trafficking, the INS has found itself involved in stopping the flow of drugs into the United States. Because illegal aliens are often employed to bring illicit narcotics across U.S. borders, the DEA trains Border Patrol agents in drug investigation and enforcement. In 1986, Border Patrol officers in California seized a shipment of 1,285 pounds of cocaine—the largest shipment ever captured by Border Patrol officers near the California-Mexico border. The officers credited their DEA training, completed only one week earlier, for their success. However, the drug problem is getting worse. In 1985, the Border Patrol captured 885 drug shipments, but between October 1987 and September 1988 it seized 3,300 shipments representing more than $700 million worth of drugs. Most of the shipments are from Central and South America, the most notorious source being the infamous Medellín drug cartel. Based in Medellín,

Baranardo Roldán (left) and Guillermo Delgado, two alleged members of the Medellín drug cartel, are held in a Colombian jail. The INS works alongside the Drug Enforcement Administration (DEA) to stop the flow of illegal drugs across U.S. borders.

The U.S. Coast Guard intercepts a rickety sailboat packed with Haitians seeking refuge in the United States. In 1981, as many as 1,000 Haitians a month began to flee the deteriorating political and economic conditions in their country. Although President Ronald Reagan ordered the Coast Guard to turn back boats carrying Haitians, INS officers were assigned to Coast Guard cutters to interview those claiming refugee status.

Colombia, this group of drug producers and distributors supplies as much as 80 percent of the world's cocaine. Although several leaders of the organization were arrested in Colombia in 1989 and extradited (surrendered by one state or authority to another) to Florida to face charges of drug smuggling, the illegal drug traffic continues virtually unchecked.

In recent years, the INS has also been confronted with the problem of boat people (people who flee their homeland, often due to war or oppression, in overcrowded boats) from Vietnam, Cuba, and Haiti. The Cuban crisis demonstrates the difficulties that boat people present for the INS. In 1980, Cuban leader Fidel Castro expelled about 125,000 Cubans from the city of Mariel, and many of the "Marielitos" arrived on the Florida coast. American officials ultimately accepted most of the refugees, the majority of whom settled in Florida. But it soon became apparent that a large number of convicts were among the boatloads of Cubans. The INS immediately arrested and detained many of them. Other Marielitos were also arrested for committing crimes after arriving in America and were detained along with the hardened criminals. Furthermore, because they were not admitted into the United States with legal status, the Marielitos were denied legal representation and the due process that is guaranteed to U.S. citizens and resident aliens. When lawyers acting for the detainees sued the government, the federal courts ultimately ruled that although the detainees were free to return to Cuba at any time, the United States was within its rights to imprison them indefinitely.

The hopelessness and frustration of the prisoners came to a head late in 1987, when they learned that U.S. officials had reached an agreement with

Cuban detainees at the INS detention center in Oakdale, Louisiana, unfurl a banner directed at President Ronald Reagan. Cuban inmates, fearing reprisals if they were returned to Cuba, seized control of the Oakdale facility and the federal penitentiary in Atlanta, Georgia, in November 1987. The detainees relinquished control of the facilities when Attorney General Edwin Meese III promised that each of their cases would be reviewed individually.

Cuba to deport more than 2,500 of them. Desperate not to be returned to their native country, where many of them had feared for their life, the Cubans seized control of two of the prisons in which they were held—the INS medium-security detention center in Oakdale, Louisiana, and the federal penitentiary in Atlanta, Georgia. The inmates took over the Oakdale facility first, taking hostages and setting fire to buildings in the compound. Thirty-six hours later the Atlanta prison erupted with violence. A total of 122 hostages were held in the 2 prisons. The inmates were considered to be particularly dangerous because they had nothing to lose, and, consequently, Attorney General Edwin Meese III and prison officials decided to wait rather than storm the facility and risk lives. Demanding total amnesty (forgiveness for the incident) and the assurance that they could remain in the United States, the inmates eventually accepted Meese's promise that each of their cases would be reviewed individually. Any detainee who had only committed a minor offense, had strong family ties in America, and had stayed out of trouble while in prison would not be deported. By the end of 1988, the INS had reviewed 4,400 cases, resulting in the release of nearly 2,500 Cuban detainees.

Many officials believed that the incident was avoidable. An official of the Reagan administration said anonymously: "Our friends with the Immigration and Naturalization Service were going to send them back regardless of what crime they had committed. That's what made the Cubans so mad and, you know what, we don't blame them." Marvin Shoob, a federal judge who had presided over several cases involving Marielitos, added, "If we had fair hearings in 1981 and 1982, we never would have reached this point." The treatment of the Marielitos has brought attention to the harsh manner in which some detainees are treated. The Reagan administration in 1981 changed the process by which it handled aliens whose legal status is uncertain. Although aliens were previously paroled while they waited for a hearing, they are now immediately locked up, sometimes indefinitely. Lawyers for these prisoners claim that such treatment is actually punishment, and many aliens held in this way are losing their faith in America as a place where they can escape the often brutal problems in their native lands. Still, the desire to allow as many immigrants into America as possible must be tempered with the need to curb, as former attorney general Meese put it, "the huge waves of illegal immigrants that have put an enormous strain on many communities." Both arguments have their merits, and one of the future challenges for the INS will be to balance the two sides as fairly as possible.

In 1986, Congress passed the Immigration Reform Control Act (IRCA), a sweeping immigration reform plan that provided a one-time amnesty for

A poster advertising the legalization (amnesty) program of the 1986 Immigration Reform and Control Act (IRCA). The INS processed more than 3 million applications for temporary residence status under the program.

millions of people who were already economically integrated into American society and that sought to curb the flow of aliens entering the country illegally by making it more difficult for them to find work. Although the act met with much resistance—the bill was nearly defeated in Congress—it ultimately was adopted because it was, according to INS commissioner Alan C. Nelson, "an idea whose time had come." From a budgetary standpoint, deporting the vast number of illegal aliens would not be cost-effective.

IRCA contains two major provisions: a legalization (or amnesty) program and sanctions for employers who hire undocumented aliens. During an application period that ran between May 1987 and May 1988, any illegal alien who lived continuously in the United States since before January 1, 1982, had no serious police record, had passed a medical examination, and could prove he or she was

RESIDENT ALIEN
U.S. Department of Justice-Immigration and Naturalization Service
GARCIA-LOPEZ, ROSA MARIA
052356
A33500000
LOS NP1

An alien registration card ("green card"). The INS issues green cards to aliens who have been granted permanent resident status. Permanent residents enjoy all the rights and privileges of citizens, except that they cannot hold U.S. passports, vote, or leave the country for more than one year without losing their permanent resident status. Approximately 10 million aliens hold green cards.

financially responsible was eligible to become a legal temporary resident. (There was a separate but similar program for illegal aliens working in agriculture; the application period ran from June 1987 to November 1988.) After 18 months, a temporary resident could become a permanent resident if he or she could demonstrate a basic understanding of the English language and American history. A permanent resident could then seek U.S. citizenship through the naturalization process.

IRCA represents a major breakthrough for undocumented aliens who had been part of the American economy for years but who were unable to enjoy the benefits of legal residents. When President Reagan signed IRCA into law, his words echoed this sentiment: "[The law will] go far to improve the lives of a class of individuals who now must hide in the shadows, without access to many of the benefits of a free and open society. Very soon, many of these men and women will be able to step into the sunlight and, ultimately, if they choose, they may become Americans." To handle the large number of amnesty applications, the INS established 107 legalization offices in 32 states. A total of 3,070,000 illegal aliens participated in the program.

IRCA also prohibits employers from hiring aliens who have not been lawfully admitted into the country. Employers profit from hiring illegal aliens because they are usually willing to work for much lower wages than American laborers and because employers do not have to provide illegal aliens with health benefits or safe working conditions. The employment of illegal aliens harms both American citizens, who are shut out of employment opportunities, and illegal aliens, who are often forced to work under conditions that are barely tolerable. IRCA penalizes employers who knowingly hire undocumented aliens. These penalties range from a fine of $250 for a first offense up to $10,000 (per illegal alien) for repeated offenses. In cases where a pattern or practice of hiring illegal aliens is evident, the employer can be imprisoned for 6 months and fined up to $3,000 per violation.

IRCA also requires employers to keep more complete and accurate records of their workers. For every new employee, employers must secure official proof—such as an American birth certificate, American passport, or valid alien registration card (more commonly known as a green card)—that the person is eligible to work in the United States. The act places a substantial burden on employers because they must be careful not to hire anyone unauthorized to work and yet (because of an antidiscrimination provision) must also avoid improperly rejecting a prospective employee solely because of alien status or national origin.

Coming to America

Far more people want to come to America than the law will allow, and aliens face many barriers in attempting to immigrate to the United States. As of 1989, the State Department grants 270,000 immigration visas each year, with no more than 20,000 going to citizens of any one country. This 20,000-person-per-year limit often results in very long waiting lists for citizens of countries where the demand for immigration to the United States is high. For example, in order for a citizen of Mexico or the Philippines to have immigrated in 1988, he or she must have applied for permission in 1976. For citizens of other countries, however, the wait is shorter.

Congress has established a system that ranks applicants from each country. A six-tiered system places each applicant in one of the tiers according to his or her skills or kinship to U.S. citizens. The preference categories (and the maximum number admitted under each one) are as follows:

1. Unmarried sons and daughters (over age 21) of U.S. citizens (20 percent, or 54,000, per year).

2. Spouses and unmarried sons and daughters (along with their spouses) of permanent residents (26 percent, or 70,200, per year).

3. Members of the professions, scientists, and artists (10 percent, or 27,000, per year).

4. Married sons and daughters (over age 21) of U.S. citizens (10 percent, or 27,000, per year).

5. Brothers and sisters of U.S. citizens (24 percent, or 64,800, per year).

6. Skilled or unskilled workers needed in the United States (10 percent, or 27,000, per year).

This system allows people with relatives in the United States and those with special talents to enter the country before those without family ties or skills. If the 270,000 visas are not depleted by immigrants falling into the preference categories, other immigrants may be granted the remaining visas (a situation that has not occurred since 1978.)

In addition to the 270,000 people allowed to immigrate under the preference system, many more are allowed into the country. In 1988, more than 600,000 immigrants were admitted into the United States because they were immediate family members of U.S. citizens (or permanent residents) or were granted refugee status. Immediate family members (defined as husbands, wives, parents, and children under 21 years of age) of a U.S. citizen are automatically eligible to immigrate. The law places no limit on the number of immediate relatives who can enter.

The total number of immigrants each year is also increased by refugees whom the government allows to enter. The flow of refugees—people displaced from, or persecuted in, their native countries—is restricted by an annual quota of 50,000, but the quota is flexible to reflect the changing world situation. Every fall the attorney general, the secretary of state, and the president meet to decide how many extra refugees—over and above the 50,000 mark—will be allowed into the country the following year. Deciding who is a refugee is a very sensitive issue. Legally, the attorney general determines who qualifies for refugee status on a case-by-case basis. However, the attorney general usually

In 1988, Michelle Zere welcomes Alex Lobov, her husband of four months, as he arrives at New York's John F. Kennedy International Airport from the Soviet Union. Under immigration law, spouses of U.S. citizens are automatically eligible to enter the country irrespective of immigration quotas.

delegates this authority to the INS, which makes the actual decision in consultation with the State Department.

The process of permanent immigration to the United States typically begins when a sponsor petitions the INS for a visa on behalf of a beneficiary in a foreign country. For example, an American parent would sponsor an unmarried

95

Two immigrants are sworn in as naturalized citizens of the United States. Examiners in the Adjudications and Naturalization division of the INS check the veracity of naturalization applications submitted by permanent residents and recommmend to courts whether the permanent resident should be naturalized.

foreign-born son or daughter over 21 years old. The beneficiary would fall in the first preference category. A permanent resident sponsoring a foreign spouse would fall under the second preference category, and so on. Because the sponsor usually resides in the United States, INS officers in the Examinations division will review the petition in this country. They will confirm the sponsor's credentials as an American citizen or permanent resident and make sure that the sponsor's relationship to the beneficiary is legitimate. Because the State Department ultimately grants visas, its staff will also check the veracity of the petition, usually in the foreign country, and decide whether the beneficiary meets the requirements of immigration law. If State Department officials, in conjunction with INS officials, determine that the petition is in order, the visa is granted, and the beneficiary is allowed entry into the United States.

At the point of entry, INS officers review the credentials of the prospective immigrant once again to ensure that nothing was overlooked during the petition process that would exclude the alien from entering the United States. If the prospective immigrant's credentials are found to be valid upon landing in the United States, he becomes a permanent resident. The immigrant then receives an alien registration card that certifies legal status. On the other hand, if the alien is excluded, he can appear before an immigration judge or appeal to the administrative appeals unit in the Adjudications and Naturalization division and plead his case for remaining in America. If this fails, the alien can take his case one step further to the Board of Immigration Appeals. If he is still unsuccessful, he can take his case to the federal court of appeals. If all of the appeals fail, the alien is excluded, which means that he is not officially allowed entry and must leave the country.

After living in the United States for five years, the permanent resident becomes eligible for American citizenship by applying for naturalization. The application for naturalization is made to the INS through the Adjudications and Naturalization division, which recommends to state and federal courts whether the application should be approved. It is the courts, acting on this recommendation, that formally grant approval and administer the oath of citizenship. Once the oath is taken, the former alien becomes an American citizen with all the rights guaranteed by the Constitution.

Fireworks explode around the Statue of Liberty in New York harbor during the finale of the unveiling ceremony at the centennial celebration of the statue in 1986. Although the United States remains a land of freedom and opportunity, the INS shoulders the difficult responsibility of enforcing immigration policies that limit the number of immigrants.

SIX

Keepers of the Flame

Over the 1986 Fourth of July weekend, America celebrated its heritage as the land of opportunity. The occasion was the 100th birthday of the Statue of Liberty. A gift from the French government in 1886, the statue had welcomed immigrants entering New York harbor for a century. And now all of America, it seemed, turned out to celebrate Miss Liberty's birthday. People from all over the country descended upon New York City to join the festivities, which included a regatta of tall ships from around the world, a dazzling display of fireworks, and a rededication of the statue by President Ronald Reagan. Upon turning on the lights of the statue, he proclaimed "We are the keepers of the flame of liberty; we hold it high tonight for the world to see." In a ceremony televised from Ellis Island, Chief Justice Warren Burger led 16,000 newly naturalized American citizens in reciting the pledge of allegiance to the United States.

The Statue of Liberty serves as an enduring reminder to the world that the United States has always been a haven for the downtrodden. However, the United States remains ambivalent toward immigrants. The nation cannot forget its immigrant roots, yet it embraces policies that restrict immigration. Walking the tightrope between the fundamental ideological commitment to the less fortunate peoples of the world and the constraints of a country that many believe is filled to capacity is a monumentally difficult task.

A number of new crises, exemplified by the large number of people seeking asylum, are straining the resources of the INS. Asylum is a special status granted to aliens already in the United States who can prove a well-founded fear of persecution if they were to be returned to their homeland. Decided on a case-by-case basis (there is no limit to the number of people who can be granted asylum), asylum status allows an alien to remain in the United States; if asylum is denied, the alien is deported.

The treatment of citizens of Nicaragua and El Salvador serves as a good example of the problems surrounding asylum policy. Both Central American countries have been devastated in recent years by civil war, and a large number of Nicaraguans and Salvadorans have sought asylum in the United States. In 1987 alone, Attorney General Edwin Meese III granted asylum to 200,000 Nicaraguans. Salvadorans, however, have not been as fortunate. Tens of thousands of Salvadorans have been denied asylum, prompting critics to claim political favoritism on the part of the government, which supports the rebel factions in Nicaragua and the ruling government in El Salvador.

In a 6-month span from the end of 1988 to the beginning of 1989, there were 40,000 requests for asylum by Central Americans, as opposed to 407 in all of 1987. The processing center in Brownsville, Texas, where many of them enter the country, was so congested that INS officials had to build a tent city to detain those denied entry. Much to the dismay of the INS, those who undertake the harrowing journey to the border and brave the long lines at the processing facilities only to be turned back see illegal entry as their only option. As reported in *Newsweek* magazine, a Nicaraguan woman who was turned away with her two children at Brownsville summed up these sentiments by stating, "I will come back, but this time I will not present myself to the authorities."

The United States continually seeks new solutions to immigration problems. Its newest program is the immigration lottery. Originally part of the 1986 Immigration Reform and Control Act, the lottery system provided an extra 30,000 immigration visas (above and beyond the existing annual quota of 270,000) by 1991. The lottery was opened to citizens of countries that the United States felt were underrepresented in the current quota system, typically people from Europe, Africa, and South America. In addition, lottery applicants would be people who did not fall into one of the six preference categories. More than 1.4 million people applied for the 10,000 positions, which were filled on a first-come, first-served basis. However, the rules of the lottery permitted applicants to submit up to 1,000 applications each. This provision benefited the well-organized Irish, who were granted 4,000 of the first 10,000 visas. To close loopholes like this one, the State Department held

100

Five aliens show their new temporary resident identification cards issued by the INS. After years of living as illegal aliens, they applied for amnesty under the Immigration and Control Act of 1986 and will become eligible for permanent residency. The INS continues to assist aliens who wish to become U.S. citizens.

a second lottery in 1989 and accepted only one application per person. This second lottery awarded an additional 10,000 visas in both 1989 and 1990. A spokesperson for the State Department, which supervised the second lottery, commented, "The United States is offering immigration opportunities to a wide range of people from around the world who otherwise would never qualify."

Opportunities for economic advancement and personal freedom have attracted immigrants to the United States for nearly four centuries, and it seems unlikely that the attraction will fade as long as war, poverty, and political oppression exist in the world. Yet the United States, too, is challenged with the ever-increasing problems of poverty and despair within its own borders. The fundamental task of the nation's immigration policy, today and in the future, will be to balance the interests of the American people and prospective immigrants.

Immigration and Naturalization Service
DEPARTMENT OF JUSTICE

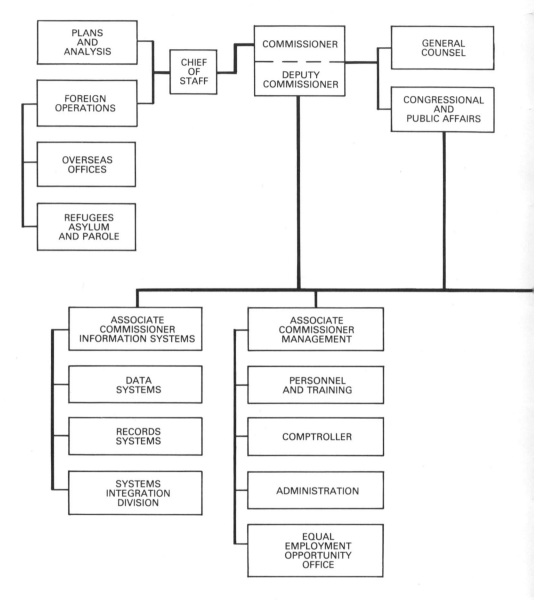

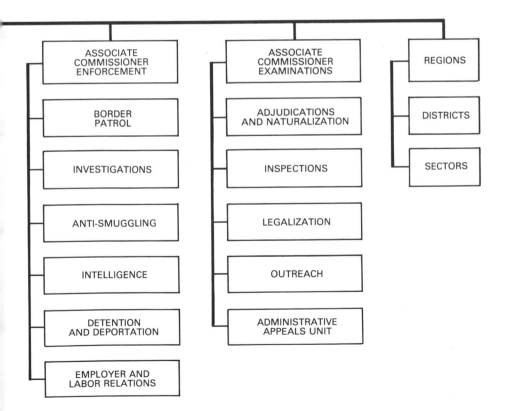

ASSOCIATE COMMISSIONER ENFORCEMENT	ASSOCIATE COMMISSIONER EXAMINATIONS	REGIONS
BORDER PATROL	ADJUDICATIONS AND NATURALIZATION	DISTRICTS
INVESTIGATIONS	INSPECTIONS	SECTORS
ANTI-SMUGGLING	LEGALIZATION	
INTELLIGENCE	OUTREACH	
DETENTION AND DEPORTATION	ADMINISTRATIVE APPEALS UNIT	
EMPLOYER AND LABOR RELATIONS		

GLOSSARY

Alien Registration Card (green card)   An identity card attesting the permanent resident status of an alien in the United States.

Asylum   Special status granted to aliens already in the United States who can prove a well-founded fear of persecution if they were to return to their homeland. Asylum status allows an alien to remain in the United States.

Border Patrol   A division of the INS that patrols the U.S. borders to ensure that no one enters the United States without following the proper procedures and apprehends those who have managed to enter the country illegally.

Contract worker   A foreign worker who has signed a contract for work in the United States for a specific period of time.

Deportation   The legal expulsion of an undocumented, or otherwise illegal, alien from the United States.

Immigration   The act of entering a country to establish permanent residence.

Immigration Reform and Control Act (IRCA)   A law passed in 1986, aimed at curbing illegal immigration by penalizing employers who hire undocumented aliens. The law also included an amnesty program for aliens who had been in the United States before January 1982.

Indentured servant   A person who has bound himself or herself to work for another person for a specified time in return for payment of travel and living expenses.

Nativism   An anti-immigrant movement in the 19th century. Nativists were eager to restrict immigration severely and to eliminate the participation of immigrants in the political affairs of the country.

Naturalization   The official process by which people acquire citizenship in a country other than the nation of their birth.

Preference category   One of the six tiers into which a prospective immigrant falls, according to his or her skills or kinship to a U.S. citizen. The State Department uses the preference category system to determine which applicants are most qualified to receive immigration visas.

Refugee   A person who flees to a foreign country because he or she has been persecuted or has a well-founded fear of persecution, on account of his or her race, religion, nationality, membership in a particular social group, or political opinions.

Restrictionist   A person who advocates the severe limitation of the number of immigrants allowed to enter the United States.

Visa   An official permit issued by the relevant authorities that allows legal entrance into a country.

SELECTED REFERENCES

Dunn, Lynne. *The Department of Justice*. New York: Chelsea House, 1989.

Kennedy, John F. *A Nation of Immigrants*. New York: Harper & Row, 1964.

Martin, George. *Madam Secretary: Frances Perkins*. Boston: Houghton Mifflin, 1976.

Reimers, David M. *The Immigrant Experience*. New York: Chelsea House, 1989.

Rips, Gladys Nadler. *Coming to America: Immigrants from Southern Europe*. New York: Laurel Leaf Books, 1981.

Select Commission on Immigration and Refugee Policy. *U.S. Immigration Policy and the National Interest*. Washington, DC: Government Printing Office, 1981.

Thernstrom, Stephen, et al., eds. *The Harvard Encyclopedia of American Ethnic Groups*. Cambridge: Harvard University Press, 1980.

Tyler, Alice Felt. *Freedom's Ferment: Phases of American Social History from the Colonial Period to the Outbreak of the Civil War*. New York: Harper & Row, 1944.

U.S. Department of Justice. Immigration and Naturalization Service. *Immigration and Naturalization Service Annual Report*. Washington, DC: Government Printing Office, 1987.

U.S. Department of Justice. Immigration and Naturalization Service. *The Immigration Border Patrol*. Washington, DC: Government Printing Office, 1952.

U.S. Department of the Interior. National Park Service. *Statue of Liberty National Monument*. Washington, DC: Government Printing Office, 1985.

Wittke, Carl. *We Who Built America: The Saga of the Immigrant*. Cleveland: Case Western Reserve University Press, 1939.

INDEX

Adams, John, 26
Adjudications and Naturalization division, 74–77, 97
AFL-CIO, 62
Alien and Sedition Acts (1798), 26
Alien Registration Act (1940), 58
American Bar Association, 62
American Brotherhood, 30
American Federation of Labor, 43, 62
American Protective Association, 43
American Revolution, 24
Anarchists Act of 1918, 53
Angel Island, 43
Attorney general, 69, 94–95

Bangkok, 72
Bedini, Gaetano, 33
Bering Strait, 21
Bingham, Theodore, 39
Board of Immigration Appeals, 75, 97
Border Patrol, 78–79, 83, 85–87
Brotherhood of Locomotive Firemen, 48
Brownsville, Texas, 100
Buchanan, James, 31
Burger, Warren, 99
Burlingame Treaty of 1868, 37
Bush, George, 64

Cabot Lodge, Henry, 42, 50
California, 37, 87
Canseco, José, 16
Castle Garden, 37, 45
Castro, Fidel, 88
Charles II, king of England, 22
Chief of Staff, Office of the, 69, 71–73

China, 37, 59
Chinese Exclusion Act of 1882, 43, 60
Civil War, U.S., 35
Cleveland, Grover, 50
Colombia, 88
Columbus, Christopher, 21
Comptroller, Office of the, 82
Congress, U.S., 16, 25–27, 30, 37–38, 41–45, 48, 50–51, 52, 55–56, 57, 61–62, 64, 65, 73, 90, 93
Congressional and Public Affairs, Office of, 69, 73, 75
Congress of Industrial Organizations, 62
Constitution, U.S., 25, 38
Cuba, 88–90
Czolgosz, Leon, 45

Daughters of the American Revolution, 62
Declaration of Independence, 24, 25, 33
Delaware, 22
Democratic party, 30
Democratic-Republican party, 26
Denmark, 28
Department of Commerce and Labor, 45
Deportation Act of 1919, 53
Detention and Deportation division, 79–80, 83
Dillingham, William P., 51
Dillingham Commission, 51
Displaced Persons Act (1948), 60–61
Drug Enforcement Administration (DEA), 77, 79, 87

Einstein, Albert, 16
Ellis Island, 15–16, 45, 99

El Salvador, 100
England, 21, 22, 28
Executive Office for Immigration Review, 75
Executive Order 6166, 57

Federal Bureau of Investigation (FBI), 58, 77, 79
Federalist party, 26
Fillmore, Millard, 31
Foran Act, 43
Foreign Operations, Office of, 71, 72
France, 21, 26
Frances Cabrini, Saint, 16
Frémont, John C., 31
French and Indian War, 22
French Revolution, 26

General Counsel, Office of the, 69, 71
General Counsel's Law Bulletin, The, 71
George III, king of England, 24
Georgia, 22
Germany, 28
Gompers, Samuel, 43
Grant, Madison, 39

Haiti, 88
Harding, Warren, 54
Harrison, Benjamin, 44
Hart-Celler Act, 63–64
Henderson v. Mayor of New York (1876), 37
Hoover, Herbert, 57
House Committee on Immigration, 56

Immigration
  arrival of southern Europeans and, 38–40
  asylum and, 100
bracero program and, 59–60
colonial period and, 21–23
discrimination and, 22–23, 25–26, 29–33, 37, 38–40, 43
drug smuggling and, 79, 87–88
illegal, 19, 64–66, 77–79, 85–87
literacy test and, 49–52
need for labor and, 36
process of, 95–97
quotas for, 19, 55, 63, 93–94
refugees and, 94–95
religion and, 28, 30, 32, 33
state legislation and, 36–37
Immigration, Bureau of, 35, 45
Immigration Act of 1882, 41
Immigration Act of 1917, 52, 57
Immigration and Nationality Act. *See* McCarran-Walter Act
Immigration and Naturalization, Bureau of, 48
Immigration and Naturalization Service
  creation of, 57
  description of, 69
  program areas of
    Enforcement, 77–80
    Examinations, 74, 75–77, 96
    Information Systems, 80–81
    Management, 82
  structure of, 69–83
  transfer to Justice Department of, 58
  See also Immigration
Immigration Reform and Control Act of 1986 (IRCA), 65–66, 77, 90–93, 100
Immigration Restriction League, 43
Inspections division, 74
Internal Security Act, 61
Ireland, 28
Italy, 55

Japanese Americans, 59
Jefferson, Thomas, 67
Johnson, Albert, 56
Johnson, Lyndon B., 63–64
Johnson Act (1921), 54–55
Justice Department, 58, 69, 75,
    77

Kennedy, John F., 62–63
Kenrick, Francis Patrick, 32
Know-Nothing party, 30–32,
    43

Lazarus, Emma, 15
Legalization division, 74
Lincoln, Abraham, 33, 35
Los Angeles, California, 37
Louisiana, 37

McCarran, Pat, 61
McCarran-Walter Act, 61–62,
    63
McCarthy, Joseph, 61
McKinley, William, 45, 50
Marielitos, 88–90
Marine Hospital Service, 44
Marriage Fraud Amendments
    Act of 1986, 75
Massachusetts, 30, 36–37
Medellín drug cartel, 87–88
Meese, Edwin, III, 90
Mexico, 64, 79, 93
Mexico City, 72
Mitchell, John, 43

National Automated Immigra-
    tion Lookout System
    (NAILS), 81
National Origins Act, 55–56
Nation of Immigrants, A
    (Kennedy), 62
Native American party. See
    Know-Nothing party
Naturalization Act of 1790, 25–
    26
Naturalization Act of 1795, 26

Naturalization Act of 1906, 48
Nelson, Alan C., 91
Netherlands, the, 21, 22
"New Colossus, The," 15
New Jersey, 22
Newsweek, 100
New York, 15, 22, 36, 37, 45,
    79, 99
Nicaragua, 100
Norway, 28

Oakdale Federal Alien Deten-
    tion Center, 80, 90
100 percenters, 54
Owen, William D., 44

Passing of the Great Races
    (Grant), 39
Penn, William, 22
Pennsylvania, 22, 28, 30
Perkins, Frances, 57
Philippines, 93
Pius IX, 33
Plans and Analysis, Office of,
    71
Portugal, 21

Rajneesh, Bhagwan Shree, 77–
    78
Reagan, Ronald, 59, 64, 92, 99
Refugee Act (1980), 64
Refugees, Asylum, and Parole,
    Office of, 71–72
Republican party, 30–31, 35
Rome, Italy, 72
Roosevelt, Franklin, 57, 58
Roosevelt, Theodore, 48, 50, 53
Ross, Edward A., 39

San Francisco, California, 37,
    43
Sargent, Frank, 48–49
Second Continental Congress,
    24
Section 24 squad, 57
Shannon, Ireland, 73

Shoob, Marvin, 90
Sons of the Sires of '76, 30
Spain, 21
Special Assistant United States
    Attorneys Program, 71
State Department, 35, 72, 93,
    95, 96, 101
Statue of Liberty, 15, 99
Supreme Order of the Star-
    Spangled Banner, 30
Sweden, 28

Taft, William Howard, 51
Treasury Department, 41, 44,
    45, 77, 82
Truman, Harry, 62

United Mine Workers, 43
United States Customs Service,
    77
Ursuline Convent, 33

Vietnam, 88

Walter, Francis, 61
War Brides Act (1946), 60–
    61
Washington, George, 19, 67
Whig party, 30
Wilson, Woodrow, 52
World War I, 52–53
World War II, 59–61

Edward H. Dixon, a researcher and writer, holds a B.A. in history from Columbia University. He has contributed to books on U.S. history and politics and is currently writing a book about baseball. He lives in Washington, D.C.

Mark A. Galan, a chemist turned historical researcher and writer, holds a B.A. in chemistry from Columbia University. He has worked on projects ranging from astrophysics to popular culture. He lives in Alexandria, Virginia.

Arthur M. Schlesinger, jr., served in the White House as special assistant to Presidents Kennedy and Johnson.He is the author of numerous acclaimed works in American history and has twice been awarded the Pulitzer Prize. He taught history at Harvard College for many years and is currently Albert Schweitzer Professor of the Humanities at the City College of New York.

PICTURE CREDITS